FOR WOMEN WHO DARE TO BE GIRLS
FOR MEN WHO WANT TO UNDERSTAND THEM

For a period of modern time bounded roughly by the birth control pill and the Betamax, female human beings transformed themselves into no-nonsense dynamos called women. The girl was banished. There was no such thing as a girl.

Now we are entering another phase in the history of women. Women are rediscovering the girl-inside-the-woman. They are laughing at her rituals, applauding her persistence. They are touched by her bravery. They are moved by her dignity.

The girl, it turns out, never disappeared at all. The best of her was there all the time.

The girl has been rescued and *The Secret Life of Girls* is her story.

LESLEY DORMEN has been an editor at *American Girl* magazine. Her articles and essays appear in *Mademoiselle* and *McCall's* magazines, and she is working on a collection of short stories. MARK ZUSSMAN has been an editor at *Esquire* and *Oui* magazines. He is working on *A Grown-Up Children's Guide to Their Parents,* and his critical study of Jane Austen will be published in the spring.

THE SECRET

Lesley Dormen

Illustrations by
Debra Solomon

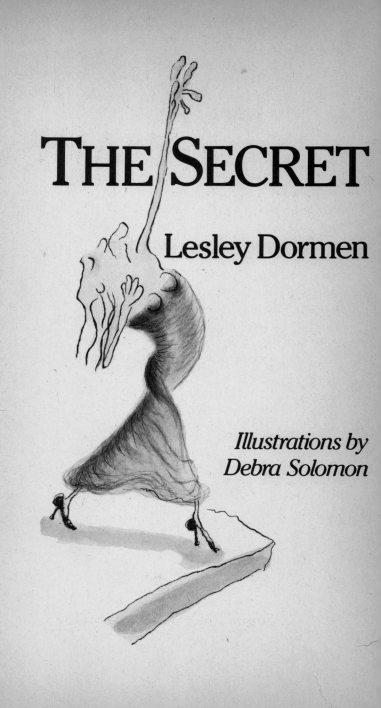

LIFE OF GIRLS

and Mark Zussman

A PLUME BOOK

NEW AMERICAN LIBRARY

NEW YORK AND SCARBOROUGH, ONTARIO

PLUME TRADEMARK REG. U.S. PAT. OFF. AND FOREIGN COUNTRIES
REGISTERED TRADEMARK—MARCA REGISTRADA
HECHO EN HARRISONBURG, VA., U.S.A.

SIGNET, SIGNET CLASSIC, MENTOR, PLUME, MERIDIAN and NAL
BOOKS are published *in the United States* by New American Library,
1633 Broadway, New York, New York 10019, *in Canada* by The
New American Library of Canada Limited, 81 Mack Avenue,
Scarborough, Ontario MIL IM8

LIBRARY OF CONGRESS CATALOGING IN PUBLICATION DATA
Dormen, Lesley.
  The secret life of girls.
  1. Girls—Anecdotes, facetiae, satire, etc.
I. Zussman, Mark.   II. Title.
PN6231.G5D67   1984   818'.5402   84-8345
ISBN 0-452-25508-2

First Printing, July, 1984

1 2 3 4 5 6 7 8 9

PRINTED IN THE UNITED STATES OF AMERICA

CONTENTS

How Girls Adapted and Survived 1

Fourteen Things Every Girl's Mother Told Her 2

The One Thing Every Girl's Father Told Her 3

What Girls Expect of New Year's Eve 4

The General Theory of Girl Hygiene 6

The General Theory of Girl Upkeep 8

What's Inside a Girl's Purse 9

Why a Girl Can't Leave More Stuff at Home 11

Girls and Mirrors 12

Girls and Makeup 15

Why a Girl Never Has As Many Shoes As She Needs 16

Girls and Cotton 18

The Special Meaning of Silk in the Mind of Girls 19

Seventeen Secrets of the Girl Bottom Drawer 20

The Girl Color Spectrum 22

Thirteen Common Household Objects That Girls
Believe Are a Solution to All Problems, Terrestrial
and Extraterrestrial 23

On the Emotional Life of Girls 24

Why Girls Make Scenes 28

Nine Kinds of Girl Tears 29

The Fourteen Major Girl Lies   30

Five False Statements, Not Exactly Lies, That Girls
    Actually Believe   31

Five Girl Questions That Are Really Very Complex
    Statements   32

Why Girls Are Always "Killing Themselves" to Get
    There   33

Girls and the Telephone   34

Thirteen Things That Make a Girl Fall in Love with a
    Boy   38

Eleven Things Which, When a Girl Is Pretty Sure She
    Doesn't Want to Go to Bed with a Boy, Really Drive
    the Nail into the Coffin   39

Ten Men Girls Always Flirt With   40

Ten Men Girls Never Flirt With   41

Why Girls Love Woody Allen   42

Why Girls Love Burt Reynolds   43

Why Girls Love Joe DiMaggio   44

Girls and Gifts   45

Twelve Men Girls Know They Must Avoid Their Fatal
    Attraction To   46

What Girls Really Think about Boys' Bodies   47

Why Girls Like Sex Anyway   48

How a Girl Knows When She's Getting Her Period   50

How a Girl Knows When She's Not Getting Her Period   51

What Girls Do When They're Alone   52

Thirteen Things Girls Want to Keep You in the Dark
    About   56

The Girl Mind   58

How Girls Evaluate Evidence   62

The Special Meaning of Cuteness in the Mental Life of
Girls   63

Girls and the Weather   64

Girls and God   65

Girls and the Occult   66

Girls and History   68

Girls and Number   70

The Girl Gospel of Peace through Mutual
Understanding   71

Seventeen Girl Fears, Each More Potentially
Devastating Than Nuclear Holocaust   73

Girls and the Office   74

Girls and the Chain of Command   78

Girls in Groups   79

Girls and Food   80

Girls and Drink   83

Girls and Other People's Weddings   85

How Girls Think about Marriage   86

How Girls Vacation   88

Girls and Their Friends, Part I   90

Girls and Their Friends, Part II   91

What Girls Talk about the Morning after the Date   92

Fifteen Things Every Girl's Best Friend Tells Her   95

Bad Girls Good Girls Envy   96

Good Girls Bad Girls Wish They Were More Like   97

The Three Ways Girls Go Shopping   98

Girls and Money in General   101

Girls and the Balance of Payments   102

Girls and Foreign Money   103

Girls and Cars   104

Seventeen Names That Mean Everything to Girls   106

Eighteen Names That Mean So Much to Girls That
They Know Them Just by Their Initials   107

The Special Relationship between Girls and Cats   108

Girls and Dogs   109

Girls and Endangered Species   110

Girls and Cockroaches   111

Girls and Other People's Children   112

Girls and Children in General   113

Why Girls Have to Have *Vogue* the Day It Comes Out   114

Girls and *Cosmo*   115

Mothers As Girls   116

On the Mettle of Girls   117

THE SECRET
LIFE OF GIRLS

HOW GIRLS ADAPTED AND SURVIVED

It has commonly been thought that the girl—a female subspecies as dazzling and mysterious as the dinosaur and the saber-toothed tiger—existed as many as a million years ago, only to vanish without warning in the late twentieth century. Girls, girl nature, the girl bent, the ceremony of girls, the spectacle of girls all were assumed to have given way under the evolutionary impetus of the coed dormitory, the unisex attaché case, and the tweed jacket with suede elbow patches.

Still, girls continued somehow to exist. Even though no one was willing to answer to the name of girl, girls continued to exist in the pink blankets of hospital nurseries, in lipstick stains on whiskey sour glasses, in the living remains of scrapbooks and diaries, in the closed bathroom door, the word *cute,* the question "How much tax do I save if I have it sent to Connecticut?"

What we now know is that girls didn't disappear at all. They were just living Somewhere Else under an assumed name. Look around you. Your mother is a girl. Your sister is a girl. If you're a boy, your girl friend is a girl. If you're a girl, you're a girl. Barbara Walters is a girl.

FOURTEEN THINGS EVERY GIRL'S MOTHER TOLD HER

"Your father loves you very much; he just doesn't know how to show it."

"Get your hair out of your eyes."

"It's just as easy to marry a rich man as a poor one."

"You got that trait from your father's side of the family."

"Don't settle for second best."

"Don't be so picky."

"He's not good enough for you."

"Go anyway. You don't have to marry him."

"Show them that you come from a good home."

"Be sure you carry a dime for a phone call."

"If you squint like that, your face is going to freeze permanently in that expression."

"Remember to tell the butcher to trim the fat."

"It breaks my heart to see you living that way."

"I know you better than anyone else and I'm the only one who will tell you the truth."

THE ONE THING EVERY GIRL'S FATHER TOLD HER

"Ask your mother."

WHAT GIRLS EXPECT OF NEW YEAR'S EVE

Just when girls think they have cured themselves of the senior prom, the virus goes latent, resurfaces as New Year's Eve Disease, and lays them up for life. When the fever is at its peak—from the July Fourth weekend through the first eggnog party—urgent questions arise out of the delirium: *Who is my date? Can I get shoes dyed to match? Do we have reservations? Should I bring along the book of baby names? Is a smallpox booster required? Will there be tobogganing?* Girls hallucinate an ideal New Year's Eve involving two changes of clothing and culminating in a dawn breakfast of bacon and eggs and Dom Pérignon, preferably on a beach, preferably in another time zone. When a girl is not hallucinating, she expects only a souped up date. She expects to be allowed to get dressed up. She expects to be kissed at midnight. She expects at least one quick pass through a major downtown hotel. She expects not to have to walk home.

Unhappily, even these modest expectations suggest that the disease is exhibiting one of its most harrowing symptoms: total memory loss. History provides no evidence that any girl has ever had a good time on New Year's Eve. New Year's Eve is the occasion on which girls cry in cars, get tricked into drinking New York State champagne, get sick in strange toilets, lose valuable heirloom jewelry. If girls were able to call on experience, they would take the phone off the hook and hide under the covers.

Instead, they behave like a punch-drunk fighter who doesn't know enough to stay down for the count. Fortunately, sometime around January third the fever breaks and girls go into remission for a year, except for the occasional Saturday night flare-up.

THE GENERAL THEORY OF GIRL HYGIENE

Every girl simultaneously adheres to two distinct and utterly incompatible standards for the use of soap, pumice stone, the broom, the sponge, Q-tips, spit, and dim lighting. The first standard is inherited from her mother and is used to judge hotel bathrooms, rental car ashtrays, the tines of forks in restaurants, and the office coffeepot. The second standard, which she improvised out of attitudes she found lying around her college dormitory, is highly liberal toward the bottom rungs of chairs at her own dining table, toward shelf paper, toward dead cuticle, and toward Rome, Italy, and it closes one eye to the green slime in a boy's bathtub, at least until a relationship gets serious and one night she gets down on her knees and scrubs the thing herself.

Despite its liberalism, girl hygiene takes up an awful lot of space, especially the four corners of the bathtub, the air rights under the shower head, the windowsill, the pockets in the shower curtain, the medicine cabinet, two or three Lancôme gift totes, and the storage area under the sink where discredited hygiene products go to decompose. A girl needs all this space because she is convinced that shampoos and conditioners and protein remoisturizers periodically lose their potency, and, unless they are rotated, her hair will cease to be fluffy, bouncy, unstaticky, shiny, and thick, and she might as well go back to Cleveland where she came from.

For a time in the late seventies, girls believed that cleanliness was not next to godliness but to sexiness, which was next to healthiness, so that cleanliness contributed to sexiness and sexiness to healthiness like three cruise ship social directors all working together to make sure that everyone has a wonderful time. Later, girls decided that you either like sex or you don't, squeaky cleanness might impress Donny Osmond but it won't get Jack Nicholson to take off his sunglasses, and they either set the alarm for ten minutes later or they affected punk dishevelment. Girls also came to realize that if you clean preventively the way mothers do, rather than correctively the way normal people do, you never have the thrill of rediscovering the lost shoe under the bed or the air shaft outside the kitchen window.

THE GENERAL THEORY OF GIRL UPKEEP

A girl believes that matter, herself included, is in a constant state of decay but that ultimate dissolution can at least be slowed down a little if she pays regular visits to a cadre of sleek modern professionals—one, in charge of her anxiety level, whom she calls Doctor; another with responsibility for the length and color and general condition of her hair, whom she calls Rick; and a third, answerable for the smoothness of her legs, whom she calls Françoise and recently offered to a friend in exchange for an eyelash dyer named Anne-Marie. A girl will also give herself a certain number of treatments at home, usually in the bathroom, usually involving some combination of cotton balls, Saran Wrap, avocado halves, egg yolk, transits in and out of the shower, and maybe a kitchen timer. A girl prefers to get treatments on the outside, though, because someone will always know that she takes her coffee black and that she can or cannot stand Jane Pauley's new hairdo, as well as the precise itinerary of her forthcoming trip to Italy. Because, at any given moment, a good two-thirds of her professionals are being closely watched by the Immigration and Naturalization Service, she also gets to regale them with everything she knows about what finally happened to a Rumanian manicurist in El Cerrito. Unfortunately, just when a girl thinks that she has her treatment program settled, she always discovers something new that can be done to her—and she probably would have it done, too, and hold off disaster just that much longer, if it weren't frowned upon by society in general or forbidden outright by the FDA.

WHAT'S INSIDE A GIRL'S PURSE

"Could you just hold this a minute?"

"Sure."

"I'm trying to find my keys."

"*Love's Smoldering Ember?* 'She was a fiery bank teller trainee whose passion for a French Resistance fighter would ignite the world?' "

"Here, hold this."

"Uh, okay. How come these perfumes always sound like they got smuggled through customs under a Turkish rug?"

"I know they're in here."

"Know the feeling. Hey, I have the same sweat pants—same blow dryer, too."

"I think I hear them."

"Jeez. I didn't know they still made Pez. I see. This one has a Michael Jackson head."

"I *know* I heard them."

"Let me take that. Arctic Sunblock?"

"If I've lost my keys I'll kill myself."

"No problem. We'll find them if we have to keep at it all night. Stick that antique composition book under my arm."

"It's my diary and please don't look. Would a locksmith be open this late?"

"We could start putting stuff in my jacket pockets. Well, at least you remembered to take your diaphragm to the movies. Your passport, too? Your International Certificate of Vaccination?"

"I'm sure I had them when I left. I remember locking up."

"Let me take those . . . Italian lire dipped in red fingernail polish? And a book of French metro tickets?"

"Could you just drape these panty hose over your arm? They're clean."

"A shower cap from the Bethesda Marriott?"

"I think I've got them! Damn. These are my sister's."

"But that's great. Doesn't she have a set of yours?"

"She lives in Hawaii."

"Well, maybe we could take a break. You've got tea bags and melba toast. Maybe I can find some peanut butter and jelly in my wallet."

"Here, hold my purse. I'm going to look through my tote bag."

Sometimes when a girl is looking for something in her purse, she will set it down on the nearest clean kitchen table and empty the contents systematically: not just the diary and the diaphragm and the folding umbrella but a score of famous restaurant matchbooks, the other earring, the single glove, the sweater she lent to her best friend in high school, the white silk blouse the dry cleaner lost, maybe Jimmy Hoffa, a black hole or two, a parallel universe, a little peace and quiet, a gracious maitre d', change for a dollar. Beyond this, the work is strictly for guys in gas masks: the decaying movie ticket stubs, the decomposing Certs and Rolaids and loose birth control pills, loose tobacco and gum wrappers, and everything that didn't fit under the bathroom sink, all only barely recognizable in an inch of unexplained murky liquid.

WHY A GIRL CAN'T LEAVE MORE STUFF AT HOME

The miracle actually is not that a girl doesn't leave more stuff at home but that she can travel so far with so little—usually just one shoulder bag so heavily laden that it threatens to leave her at age thirty-two with curvature of the spine. In an ideal world, a girl wouldn't go farther than the corner coffee shop without an attendant tractor trailer containing her own bed, her own pillow, a familiar toilet seat, a boy who finds her irresistible, and the people who will always take her side even when they don't know what it is.

GIRLS AND MIRRORS

The world girls live in is a kind of archipelago of reflective surfaces in a sea of printed matter, merchandise, gadgetry, other people's faces, grilled cheese sandwiches, and so forth. The object for girls is to get from reflective surface to reflective surface without going down for the third time in the nonreflective environment. There is nothing irrational in this aspect of girl behavior. Reflective surfaces report to girls on one of the most important aspects of girl existence: They report on looks, which are girl existence.

Girls at their proficient best can coax a reflection off of anything—doorknobs, knives, store windows, train windows in tunnels, other people's eyeglasses, high-gloss conference tables, pay telephones, record album covers, white cotton sheets, walls. Mirrors are only the extreme case of reflective surfaces.

Inside every girl's head there is a map of mirror locations along

her daily route: the little triangle of mirror in the top corner of her elevator, the mirror at the entrance to the shoe store on the corner, the mirror at the exit door of her bus, the mirror behind the pie display in the deli where she buys her coffee, the mirror she has to bend a little to see behind the meats in her supermarket. In a new environment, a girl will immediately case the mirrors the way other people case the medicine cabinets or the bookshelves. When a girl gets into a boy's car for the first time and pulls down the sun visor, it does not necessarily mean that she is driving into a Colorado sunset. When she cranes across the gearshift to kiss him on the cheek, it does not necessarily mean that she is kissing him on the cheek. A girl has a distinct relationship with each mirror she looks into regularly—some mirrors are hostile to her, some ambivalent, some reassuring, some kindly. Even the worst-scenario mirror, though, has one car-

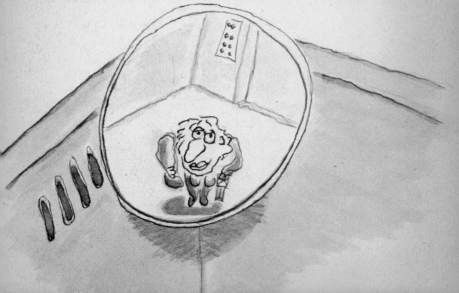

dinal virtue: it pays immediate and unremitting attention to her.

The Bureau of Standards mirror for a girl is always the mirror in her own bathroom, not because it is a sycophant but because it always conceals the truth to exactly the same degree, like a scale that always weighs ten pounds light. When a girl tries on a new item of clothing in front of the three-way mirror in a department store and *thinks* she likes it, she wants to get home fast and try it on in front of her bathroom mirror to make sure she likes it. This is why girls spend so much time standing on the rim of the bathtub.

A girl in front of a mirror is always brand-new to herself. She approaches a mirror with heightened consciousness, like a lifer going before the parole board. Two girls approach a mirror with self-conscious heightened consciousness. Two girls in a nightclub powder room apply makeup in controlled frenzy. They eye each other's equipment. They inspect each other's progress. They have primal impulses they don't quite understand. Sometimes a mirror will sneak up on an unsuspecting girl, and then she may catch a glimpse of her bad posture or, worse, her mother. After this kind of experience, a girl usually feels better if she announces, "I look terrible."

Girls know *when* to look in mirrors the same way salmon know when to swim upstream. Girls at work look in the ladies' room mirror on the way in and on the way out—and that's why they go in and out so often. In the bottom right-hand drawer of every girl's desk there is an emergency travel-size mirror which she consults to make sure she looks good enough for the trip to the ladies' room. When boys are around, a girl will look in the mirror a lot. A girl will also look in the mirror as soon as a boy has left to see how she looked from his point of view when she was with him. When mirrors are unavailable to girls—for example, when they go camping, mountain climbing, white water rafting—they pull back their hair in a barrette, substitute Chap Stick for lipstick, and let the fresh air flush their cheeks. In short, they adapt.

GIRLS AND MAKEUP

The girl relationship with makeup has always inspired thoughtful adult human beings to the deepest sorts of reflections on sham and authenticity, appearance and reality. For girls, a few difficult moments in the sixties and seventies aside, makeup has mostly been a thoughtless habit—a day-in-day-out routine of shading, highlighting, contouring, glossing, dusting, and taking care not to pull the delicate skin around the eyes. To the extent that girls bother to think about makeup philosophically, they are as likely as not to conclude that, far from concealing or hiding the true self, makeup brings out the true self and enhances it. Indeed, makeup brings out and enhances a whole gamut of true selves: one nine-to-five true self, one Saturday night date true self, a third true self for running weekend errands in the neighborhood, and a fourth, minimal true self, thrown together in a minute or so, for letting in the exterminator first thing in the morning. Girls believe that the deepest and very truest self lies buried among the tubes and jars and bottles on the main floor of the best department store in town but that it can be acquired, along with a gift tote, for $39.95 plus tax.

WHY A GIRL NEVER HAS AS MANY SHOES AS SHE NEEDS

A girl would have quite as many shoes as she needs if, when she got onto the subway at eight-thirty in the morning, she were headed not for an office but for an ice skating party, a bowling alley, a marathon, the chorus line of *42nd Street,* a rescue mission in the High Sierras, or an audition for the Andrews Sisters circa 1943. A girl gets tricked into thinking that she also has the shoes she needs for the life she actually lives because she has a lot of shoe boxes. The shoe boxes, however, have as much to do with reality as phantasms of Perrier bottles on the desert. In fact, it is an illusion that a girl has any shoes at all.

For the life she actually lives, what a girl needs are a couple of pairs of pumps, a pair of sexy sling-backs, and one decent pair of $450 glove leather boots. If a girl actually has any of these, they are recovering under a bedroom chair, drying in the hallway, or they are at the shoemaker's shop on the corner under intensive care. The boxes contain the dead and the dying: the black peau de soie evening sandal whose heel has come in and gone out of style two or three times since she bought them years ago on the off-chance that someone someday would invite her to an elegant little dinner party at the Ben Bradlees; painful reminders of the combat look, Carnaby Street, the fifties revival; relics like the Earth Shoe, the clog, the T-strap, the platform, the penny loafer; a pair of plastic jelly shoes that died in the bag as she carried them home from the store. When a girl goes shopping for a particular pair of shoes, she always has an image of those shoes in her mind, and even if she searches far and wide for those shoes, and even if she is prepared to spend the entire annual income of a Hmong tribesman for those shoes, she will see only ugly shoes and she will return home sad and frustrated and empty-handed. A girl buys a pair of shoes when she's already late for an appointment with her dentist and, as she passes a shoe store window, the very most fabulous and never-before-imagined shoes call out to her by name, and she goes in and buys them and hopes that she will be able to talk someone into stretching them so that they are very nearly her size.

GIRLS AND COTTON

Girls believe that cotton, not unlike a head of garlic worn around the neck, prevents rash, insomnia, paralysis, and untimely death, and maybe, if world leaders could learn to prefer it to polyester, it would also prevent nuclear war and continental drift. Basically girls believe cotton to be the Fred Astaire of fabrics and, in girl utopia, it would be the exclusive ingredient in mud, snakes, bad dreams, the guys on the corner, Dacron, vinyl, early-morning business meetings, and blind dates. Like certainty and Americanism, cotton, for girls, ideally comes in increments of one hundred percent. Ninety percent cotton is like a technical virgin or a little pregnant. Forty percent cotton raises the question: If God really wanted people to wash-and-wear, how come He thought up the Chinese laundry?

THE SPECIAL MEANING OF SILK IN THE MIND OF GIRLS

Girls understand silk to have properties so remarkable that, whether it is put into the hands of the same-day dry cleaner around the corner or the French specialist in whose window appears a testimonial letter from the last of the Romanovs, it can be made to vanish off the face of the earth.

SEVENTEEN SECRETS OF THE GIRL BOTTOM DRAWER

One prize-winning junior high school essay, "What Democracy Means to Me," together with one yellowing copy of the photo that appeared in her hometown newspaper after she went to Washington, D.C., to shake hands with the Senator

The bathing suit that she bought at Nice—three specks of polished cotton held together by gold ribbons—worn once, in a hotel bathroom

A nearly complete Scrabble set

A box of colored chalk

A copy of *Pat the Bunny*

Three piano technique books from the Saratoga Public Library, ten years overdue

A pair of Lucite bookends, a gift from her Aunt Louise, which, when you turn them upside down, then right them, they play "White Christmas" and snow on the village of Bethlehem

Yarn

A Depression-era glass compote, formerly her grandmother's, that she isn't sure isn't worthless

A tin Kjeldsen's imported butter cookie box containing exhaustive archival evidence of her first overseas trip, retained in case she ever becomes famous and they have to write her biography and they need to know on exactly what date in 1974 she received a cash receipt for having visited Madame Tussaud's Wax Museum

An emergency pint of Finlandia

Three broken wristwatches, one with Snow White on the face

One broken vibrator

One that works if you sort of tap it against the headboard

Ginger Rogers's autograph

A pair of diamond earrings stuffed into a sweater that she hopes will be overlooked when her apartment is robbed

A tiara

THE GIRL COLOR SPECTRUM

Nature is not the original of the girl color spectrum; the color chart is. For girls, the primary colors are not red, yellow, and blue but amber honey glaze, smoky turquoise, shimmerose, and dozens more exotic fruits, vegetables, and flowers. Girls are serially monogamous with their colors. A girl will find a color she likes, shack up with it for a year or so, then one day catch it in a cocktail lounge with every last member of the typing pool and know that it's time to reevaluate some of her basic thinking about things. Then she will find another color she likes, flirt with it for a couple of days, fly off with it for a weekend in Martinique, feel dizzy, take a deep breath, and invite it to move in. The qualities a girl likes in a good color are that it "brings out" and it "goes." If a color fails her, however, a girl, happily, has several options short of suicide: She can dye it, bleach it, exchange it, look at it only under candlelight, or add a few blond streaks.

All girls believe that all boys are color blind and that colors are useful to them only for color coding—either electrical wiring or the phones on the President's desk. Boys like to reminisce about their summer camp color wars; girls assume that, boys being boys, what they're really talking about is color clashes. Girls color-code proms (pink), weddings (white), funerals (black), first date lingerie (lavender), lunch meetings with difficult accounts (olive drab), dinner meetings with difficult boyfriends (battleship gray). When a girl says to another girl, "You could use some color," this is color code for "You need a haircut" or "You need a vacation" or "You need a nap." In the mind of girls, the absence of color isn't black; the absence of color is pale.

THIRTEEN COMMON HOUSEHOLD OBJECTS THAT GIRLS BELIEVE ARE A SOLUTION TO ALL PROBLEMS, TERRESTRIAL AND EXTRATERRESTRIAL

An extension cord

A safety pin

Baggies

Twisties

A black dress

A hint of garlic

A touch of color

Quarters and dimes

Just one puff

A Chinese take-out menu

A good super

One extra closet

Another five minutes

ON THE EMOTIONAL LIFE OF GIRLS

For girls, having an emotional life is like balancing a tower of cups and saucers on top of your head and navigating the observation deck guardrail of the Empire State Building in stiletto heels while three or four intimates try to push you off and a couple of total strangers stand below shouting, "Jump." Girls thrive on this challenge. Indeed, girls have been out on the emotional edge for so long that they have gradually moved in a complete duplicate set of makeup and enough Pepperidge Farm Goldfish to keep themselves going until a bed can be made available at Payne Whitney. Girls are never happy but they are often overjoyed; they are never sad but they are frequently suicidally depressed. Girls have read the poets and they have seen *Carmen* and *The Way We Were,* and they, too, can get an emotion off of a Grecian urn—or, for that matter, a Fiesta ware pitcher, a McDonald's commercial, a run, a snag, or a bad haircut. They can get ennui off of the guests at their mother's New Year's Day open house, compassion from Johnny Carson's having to pay such a huge alimony, or they can keep twenty or thirty of these emotions in the air at the same time, despite their ambivalence and their nausea.

The only thing girls don't like about the emotional edge is the lousy company they find there—the emotional cripples, criminals, and saints and, even farther out on the edge than they are, the scattered colonies of profoundly disturbed poet-guitarists who always want to come over with a bottle of wine and sit cross-legged on the floor and listen to Emmylou Harris records. It is not until a girl has hiked miles into the emotional flatlands that she finds a guy she'd even like to have dinner with— the successful and incredibly charming architect who just happens not to have had a feeling since 1963 when John Kennedy was shot; the amazingly handsome and articulate professional hockey

player who says, "Can't you tell I'm happy, do I have to say it?"; the enchanting mergers and acquisitions lawyer who encourages her to confess to him her deepest and most private feelings as if he were going to reciprocate and then when she's finished describes in painful detail how he was standing on the fairway of the twelfth hole when all of a sudden and so forth and so on.

When a girl has an emotion she's never felt before or she has a familiar old emotion with someone she's just met in a laundromat, she likes to savor it, turn it upside down, examine it from every possible angle, take it for a long walk in the park, talk it over with a couple of total strangers she's just met on a bus, pin a name on it, and test it to see if it survives prolonged exposure, occasional separation, and the customary two-week cooling-off period. When a girl is convinced that an emotion is authentic and not simply the kind of infatuation that she can get over in a weekend in a motel room, she takes it home with her and housebreaks it, and eventually she gets to be so comfortable with it that sometimes it can take off for two or three days at a time without her even noticing it's missing. When a girl loses control, instead of examining her emotions, she will be transported by them or swept away by them or even driven by them. When a girl is driven, she is as irreversibly embarked on a disaster course as any hero or heroine of Greek tragedy. She may try to think of something else, she may check herself into a double feature, she may try to remember how fortunate she is in so many really important ways. She knows what reason dictates, and in the very depths of her being she knows precisely what her best friends mean when they tell her, "Don't call him." And when she calls him at three in the morning, and he says, "I'm sleeping," she still gets into her car and drives one hundred and fifty miles to his mother's house and waits until it's light enough to ring the bell, and then she delivers an incoherent speech about what a wonderful person he is and how very determined she is to make things work out between them and how incredibly mild the weather is for this time of year. Driving home in a snowstorm, she feels her desperation convert to a calm, steady, blinding rage, and she is absolutely incredulous that he could have allowed her to put herself in so humiliating a position, particularly when she barely knows him.

Sometimes for a long period of time, a girl will feel no intensity of emotion at all, and she will say that she feels apathetic or affectless or pretty good, depending on the school of psychotherapy she has most recently dropped out of. She will also recognize the difference between this state and the frozenness she feels when she has a whole lot of conflicting emotions and they cancel each other out. When a girl is feeling feelingless, she will eat well, she will have all her shoes reheeled, she will feel superior to those of her friends currently in the grip of ecstasy or regret, and she will also feel vaguely horrified because she has come out of this kind of thing in the past and probably she'll come out of it this time, too.

WHY GIRLS MAKE SCENES

What gives an ordinary emotional outburst the dramatic reso-
nance of a scene is a combination of surprise, violent gesture, a
strong implication that things can never be the same again, and
the likelihood that someone will collide with a waiter on the way
out. In order to have a scene, a girl needs to be deeply emotionally involved with a passive-aggressive. She needs that passive-
aggressive to mention casually that she'd look good in a sweater
dress too if she lost ten pounds or that he'll never love anyone
the way he loved his first wife. Finally, while she hisses at him
from between clenched teeth, she needs him to sit there with
a bewildered hey-I-thought-we-were-just-out-for-a-nice-dinner
look on his face. The morning after a scene, a girl feels sick, sad,
emotionally drained, and intensely gratified, the same as after a
childhood temper tantrum. What distinguishes a scene from a
tantrum is twenty or thirty years of experience with melodrama,
docudrama, costume drama, and miniseries as well as a passing
acquaintance with Ophelia's mad scene and Thanksgiving dinner
at her mother's house. Girls tend not to make scenes in expensive
restaurants because they are intimidated by them. On the street,
however, girls make scenes regularly and a boy will know that
he is involved in a scene when a girl he thought was at his side is
in fact standing stock-still on the last corner; in a taxi, when she
demands to be let out at Twentieth Street, immediately.

NINE KINDS OF GIRL TEARS

"It seems like a second ago it was summer, and now it's bitter cold and all the leaves are dead and the trees are scraggly and in another second it will be another year, and then there'll be another year after that, and where will it all end?"

"And then he told me that I was a wonderful person with a unique character but he was pretty sure he couldn't marry a woman who didn't make him feel that he was someone else."

"No, you didn't hurt my feelings. In fact, I'm really glad you said it."

"According to my checkbook, the bank has made a terrible, terrible mistake."

"The cat died and I don't have a single spare shoe box to put it in and even if I did I'm not going to get on a plane with a dead cat and fly all the way down to Roanoke, Virginia, just so that I can bury it in my parents' backyard, and I'm not going to throw it out in the garbage either."

"No, no, no, you don't understand. *J'ai perdu mes chèques de voyage.*"

"Don't worry, you'll have my resignation on your desk first thing in the morning."

"That's the funniest thing I ever heard."

"I'm just crying, I don't have to have a reason."

THE FOURTEEN MAJOR GIRL LIES

"It was wonderful."

"How sweet of you to ask, it sounds wonderful, but I don't accept weekend dates after Tuesday night."

"Thank you very much, I'd love to."

"My momma was the first woman in the Texas State Legislature. She drank herself to death. My daddy flew his favorite plane into the side of a mountain. Then the house burned down, and lawsuits ate up all the money."

"I never knew my real parents. I was brought up in a foster home."

"After that, I went to the London School of Economics for a semester."

"We agree on everything."

"I'll have to look on my calendar."

"I had no *idea* you were going to be here."

"How incredible. That's the same direction I was going in."

"That's exactly what I think. But you put it so much better."

"You're the only person I ever told that to."

"I don't know. I've never done this before."

"I wasn't thinking about anything."

FIVE FALSE STATEMENTS, NOT EXACTLY LIES, THAT GIRLS ACTUALLY BELIEVE

"I just had to have it."

"Of course I won't tell anyone."

"I'll only be a minute."

"I don't have a thing to wear."

"All right, but just for a little while."

FIVE GIRL QUESTIONS THAT ARE REALLY VERY COMPLEX STATEMENTS

"Did you pick it out yourself?"

"Couldn't you do it just a little bit slower?"

"How do you think of such things?"

"Didn't you think Barbie looked pretty last night?"

"Won't you stay for dessert?"

WHY GIRLS ARE ALWAYS "KILLING THEMSELVES" TO GET THERE

No girl has ever been late for anything that was really important to her—basically, takeoffs and sailings. When a girl makes it to anything else on time, she is always a little disappointed that her achievement is not hailed with a ribbon-cutting ceremony, champagne, and testimonial speeches by notables. When a girl does not make it to something on time, her instinct is to brazen through the initial unpleasantness with an I-dare-you-to-say-anything-to-me glare. Force her hand, though, ask her why she's kept you waiting for three quarters of an hour in the tiny, overheated vestibule of an unheard of Greek restaurant on the South Side, and if she doesn't break down and cry, she'll explain: "First of all, it took me forever to dry my hair. Second, there weren't any cabs. And then, to top it all off, the bus never came." Raise your eyebrows a little, and she'll throw in, "Besides, the phone rang as I was going out the door." Raise your eyebrows a little further and she'll add the clincher: "It was long distance."

Deep down, girls feel so guilty about being late that the first time they came upon the book *The Late George Apley* they felt relief. "Aha," they said to themselves, "so they're not perfect either." The late girl has in fact not killed herself any less to get there late than the prompt girl has to get there on time. The way she sees it, lateness shouldn't be held against her. She has done such valiant battle against colossal forces—wet hair, hostile mirrors, traitor closets, unmailed thank-you notes, the hard-to-grasp way in which time moves forward by fits and starts—that, at several points along her route, she thought of simply not coming and consequently you're lucky to be seeing her at all.

GIRLS AND THE TELEPHONE

If you were ever to get into a serious discussion with a girl about her bare minimum requirements for the rest of her life on a desert island, she would probably tell you (after eliminating her cat, her boy friend, her television set, her subscription to *Vogue,* her clock radio, her Cuisinart, her full-length mirror, her fall wardrobe, her Bruce Springsteen records, her vanity mirror, her two best friends, and her mother), she would probably tell you that she could do it—not love it, mind you, but do it—with the contents of her large pocketbook and one Touch-Tone phone, preferably with a 32-foot cord. Allow her one more desert-island option, chances aren't bad she'd go with the Princess extension.

A girl feels about the telephone the way a boy does about a loaded revolver in the top drawer of the night table. One basic girl fantasy is having the police on 911 while an evil intruder is out in the hall, trying to pick the lock. Girls also plan emergency routes *to* the telephone. That is why, even in the smallest studio, you should not be surprised to find two instruments (a boy word, not a girl word), one by the convertible sofa and one on the wall at the crucial juncture of bathroom and kitchenette. Girls order telephones according to a formula something like the one that used to govern ordering at Chinese restaurants. At Chinese restaurants, you would order as many dishes as persons in the party, minus one. Girls order as many telephones as persons in a living space, plus one.

When a boy arrives at a girl's apartment for a date, he should not be surprised if the phone rings immediately and the girl answers and says, "I can't talk now; I'll call you back later." This

34

is a friend calling to ask if he's there yet. "I can't talk now; I'll call you back later" means yes. Girls monitor each other's personal news with the same interest that the Pentagon has in the comings and goings of Soviet submarines. This is why the phone company must love girls. Girl phone calls occur in flurries, each communication begetting a countercommunication and then a series of supplementary communications.

Girls, however, do not squander message units only on calling each other. They also call phone company services like the weather and quasi-services like horoscope. Girls shun telephone directories. Girls get their numbers from information even in cities where information sells for thirty cents a jingle. Girls complain a lot about their long-distance bills, but such complaints are not to be taken seriously. When a girl says she can't believe the call to her best friend in London cost forty dollars, she is actually making an indirect boast. Girls are *proud* of their long-distance bills—the way boys are proud of having caught a long fish. One reason that girls like the telephone is that it provides a way of spending substantial sums of money without the inconvenience of having to leave the house.

There are other differences between boys and girls in relation to the telephone. For boys, for example, the telephone is a piece of technology to be outwitted and mastered by way of blue boxes and hot wires. For girls, the telephone is a living force to be manipulated and appeased. "Please ring. Dear telephone, please ring. Ring just this once and I promise I'll never ask you for anything again." Most girls will tell you that the silent telephone makes the loudest sound they know. They will also tell you that the ringing telephone sometimes makes the loudest sound they know. When a boy wants to make a telephone not ring, he will open it up and disconnect a wire. When a girl wants to make a telephone not ring, she will bury it under pillows or take the receiver off the hook or simply unplug it. A girl wants a telephone not to ring when she is trying to catch up on her sleep or when she is entertaining a boy seriously and can't afford to be distracted.

Whereas girls don't know much about telephone wiring, they do know a lot about arcane phone company services, which for boys exist only as rumor. These services include verify-for-busy and emergency interrupt. A girl emergency might be: "It's eight-thirty and he's not here yet." Girls seem to know more than boys about the various hours at which long-distance rates change; they also act on this knowledge less.

Anyone who has called girls much in his life knows that they will pick up only after the second ring. The reason for this is that their mothers told them that they shouldn't appear too eager. No girl wants a boy to think that she's been waiting by the telephone for him even though she has. Their mothers also told them that picking up only after the second ring gives the impression that the house is larger. Any boy who has called girls much in his life knows that they have to know him pretty well before they'll admit to recognizing his voice, if he doesn't identify himself. This is why girls say, "Who *is* this?" in such a no-nonsense way. Girls play telephone the way boys play poker: close to the chest.

Girls' biggest fear about the telephone is that it will evolve out of their control. When girls think about the year 2000, they figure they can live with cloning, test-tube reproduction, and *Halloween VII*. What they figure they can't live with is the picture-telephone, for the most important reason girls like the telephone is that it provides a means of being close and even of being intimate without their first having to comb their hair and brush their teeth, though in fact most girls do comb their hair and brush their teeth before talking on the telephone. The occult reasoning behind this behavior is difficult to explain, and it may not be explainable. Most boys would not like to know what girls do while they are talking on the telephone—nor would they like to know the multitude of sins covered by the words, "Can you hold on just a minute please?"

THIRTEEN THINGS THAT MAKE A GIRL FALL IN LOVE WITH A BOY

He hopes she doesn't mind if he's a half hour late picking her up, because this is his night for reading to the blind.

He really admires people who have to make their way in the world without a trust fund.

He knows who Anne Tyler is.

He called her father "sir," unselfconsciously.

Even though he's an investment banker, deep in his heart he would really like to be a veterinarian.

On the dance floor, he has one left foot and one right foot.

He gives blood.

His sun is in Jupiter.

Her mother hates him.

He said that he once went out with Jessica Lange and, frankly, he couldn't see what all the fuss is about.

He paid for dinner with cash.

He feels sorry for men who don't want to have children.

His father is chairman of the board of the Mobil Oil Company.

ELEVEN THINGS WHICH, WHEN A GIRL IS PRETTY SURE SHE DOESN'T WANT TO GO TO BED WITH A BOY, REALLY DRIVE THE NAIL INTO THE COFFIN

He speaks of himself, in the third person, as The Kid.

His second favorite piece of music is the *William Tell* Overture, right on the heels of the theme from *Rocky*.

His favorite author is Leo Buscaglia.

His second favorite author is whoever it is that writes *Consumer Reports*.

He has five incredibly funny ways of answering the telephone: "Joe's Deli," "Chicken Ranch," "O'Grady's Funeral Parlor," "Oval Office," "Sanitation Department, Vito speaking."

He seems really curious to know her views on bondage and discipline.

Sometimes, when he thinks she isn't looking, he spreads his arms, careens from side to side, makes a whirring engine sound, and strafes an enemy village from twenty-five feet.

He knows seven different girls who would give their eye tooth to go to bed with him.

His moon is in Saturn.

Every time she says something even vaguely amusing, he winks and raises his glass and says, "Here's looking at you, kid."

He had planned all along to be a brain surgeon, but he finally realized that by going into animal husbandry he could serve humanity better.

TEN MEN GIRLS ALWAYS FLIRT WITH

The butcher

Cab drivers

Her brother

Bartenders

Her brother's best friend

Her boss's boss

Her hair stylist

The vet

The guy at the garage if he's not older than twenty-seven

Cops

TEN MEN GIRLS NEVER FLIRT WITH

The gynecologist

The Chinese food deliveryman

Office messengers

Her best friend's boyfriend

Her boss

The divorced guy on three who wears gold chains and always says "Lookin' good" no matter what, even if she's not looking good and even if he's got his date with him

The super

The mailman

The dentist

Any man who works in a department store

WHY GIRLS LOVE WOODY ALLEN

Boys who invest their energy and much of their free time in developing biceps and pectorals are always mystified when the girl walks off into the sunset—admittedly, a polluted urban sunset—with a manically gesticulating 98-pound wimp. What the body builder boys don't understand is that girls love Woody Allen because, even though he represents himself on screen as a cowardly, insecure neurotic, he is in fact a fabulously gifted artist with a spectacular Fifth Avenue apartment, enough money to finance any project, however moronic, and immediate access to any celebrity he has an impulse to talk to—besides which, no matter what indignities he might imagine himself the victim of, no one would so much as dream of putting him on hold. Girls also like Woody Allen for his ability to combine talk with all other human activities: eating, walking, waiting around, hanging out, having sex—maybe even sleep, utter silence, and death. As for the body builder boys, they don't seem to grasp that biceps are all but worthless in modern cities; whatever the theoretical risks of enemy ambushes and runaway snowplows, on a day-to-day basis the big challenge is choreographing the next twelve hours to accommodate the accountant, the lawyer, the psychiatrist, a few chapters of Kierkegaard, and lunch at the Russian Tea Room.

WHY GIRLS LOVE BURT REYNOLDS

Ever since girls fell for Woody Allen, scrawny neurotic boys have had such an exaggerated sense of their own seductiveness that they cannot believe it—and indeed feel that fundamental rules of the game have been changed on them—when the girl walks off into the sunset with a 220-pound beefcake heartthrob who doesn't walk into walls and doesn't hide behind the dune when they're choosing up teams for volleyball. What the scrawny neurotic boys don't understand is that the killer brutes have not only taken Introduction to Poetry and Modern Italian Cinema at Ohio State University, they have also caught which way the wind is blowing and they have added to their own outsize virtues a large measure of Woody Allen self-awareness, sensitivity, and angst. Any boy who has trouble understanding this process should give a little thought to the way in which General Motors has learned to pass off its own oversized monsters as Toyotas, Datsuns, and Peugeots.

WHY GIRLS LOVE JOE DIMAGGIO

Girls love Joe DiMaggio because, whenever he comes onto the television screen for Mr. Coffee or some desperate down-at-the-heels savings bank, they know that, all the time he's smiling there and being so dignified, inside he's really still all torn up by the agonizing memory of his one great love, Marilyn Monroe. Girls think that, if they could only get him alone for a little while, they might be able to soothe him and make him suffer less, and also they might be able to get him to tell them all kinds of neat things about what it was like when Dwight D. Eisenhower was president and Calvin Klein was still wearing blue jeans with somebody else's name on them and you couldn't get fresh pasta any time you wanted it.

GIRLS AND GIFTS

Girls give gifts; they receive presents. The logic of this is simple: Presents have ribbons attached, gifts have strings. A girl, in other words, does not mind dishing out obligation but she would just as soon not take it on. Although girls are familiar with, and even open to the idea, that what really counts in any offering is the thought, thought is never altogether real to them until it is made manifest in scents, lingerie, fur, precious metals, or gems. Girls believe that when a man gives you a gift, it means that he's been paying attention and grasped a few subtleties and not misunderstood when you said that the opal in the window was kind-of-nice or okay or not-exactly-my-kind-of-thing or that the rhinestone earrings were really fabulous but you couldn't wear them as many places as the tiny diamond studs. Girls also believe that good things come in small packages, but then they've got to be really good. Girls welcome and even expect flowers but never mistake them for presents, and the same is true of dinners and theater tickets, even really good seats. Other things that girls consider marginal as presents are shower massagers, kitchen appliances, English soaps, posters, gift certificates for hair analysis, and reference books. Although a girl will always appreciate the cleverness and uniqueness of surprise activities designed especially for her amusement—a mystery ride at the end of which go-go boys emerge out of a cake and a plane overhead skywrites HAPPY BIRTHDAY—a boy should not be surprised if she sulks later on. A girl likes opening boxes.

TWELVE MEN GIRLS KNOW THEY MUST AVOID THEIR FATAL ATTRACTION TO

Minor celebrities, particularly TV sportscasters and drummers who claim to be close personal friends with Tommy Tune

Major celebrities with more or less limitless supplies of cocaine and a proven incapacity to memorize any other person's first or last name

Starving artists with lots of potential

Foreigners

Men who understand exactly how she feels

Potters

The guy who lectures on French cinema at the adult school and can't meet you for brunch on Sunday because he always goes to his mother's

Unhappily married borderline alcoholics

Henry Kissinger

Anyone who saves back issues of *Soldier of Fortune* magazine and knows several alternative routes between Windhoek, South-West Africa, and Silva Porto, Angola

Anyone whose name has ever appeared on a television screen on election night alongside the words PROJECTED WINNER

Underdogs

WHAT GIRLS REALLY THINK ABOUT BOYS' BODIES

Girls are very good at distinguishing between a boy's body and the boy inside of it, and they are also very good at overlooking the body for the boy or, after a couple of piña coladas and a winter of scarcity, the boy for the body. A girl writing a Harlequin romance would dress her hero up in Big Ten shoulders, narrow hips, lean, athletic legs, and she'd stuff half a box of Kleenex into his crotch. The villain, who'd appear to be triumphing until he ran into a registration problem with the SEC, would be pearish in shape, he'd have a single unsightly tuft of hair in the middle of his chest, and he'd suffer from recurrent bouts of impotence as the result of too much consensual adult homosexuality and an unrepentant negative attitude toward the women's movement. When a girl falls for a pearish boy in real life and not only is he not in trouble with the SEC, he's a rising attorney with the SEC, she attempts to draw her friends' attention to the intelligence in his one good eye, the way his socks never fall down and gather at his ankles, the determination with which he keeps ball-point pens out of his front shirt pocket, the virtual indiscernibility of his bald spot as long as he doesn't tilt his head too far forward—not to mention that when he falls asleep in front of the television sometimes you might almost mistake him for Richard Benjamin. As for the impotence, she knows that the male body is set up kind of like an overdesigned Air Force weapon system. Things do break down. But with patience, understanding, and four or five years in psychotherapy, maybe someday they'll actually be able to have sex.

WHY GIRLS LIKE SEX ANYWAY

For girls, sex is the great banquet—a lavish feast, a dazzling lineup of after-dinner speakers, and the opportunity to put aside everything they learned in Sunday school before having to go home to famine and the inevitable second thoughts. Shere Hite hands out questionnaires at the door, Helen Gurley Brown encourages and consoles, Phil Donahue defends the right of all Americans to miss the point in their own words, and Masters and Johnson promise to wire the entire Mississippi River Valley for the consummate orgasm. The only thing that bothers a girl is that the people who organize these things always advertise fancy hors d'oeuvres and duck à l'orange, then serve up ground round and mashed potatoes with a great proud smile as if it were the most delicious thing in the world. It also bothers her a little that the stranger on her left knows every last one of the truly tasteless jokes, the stranger on her right mauls her knee and tries to persuade her to drive to Atlantic City with him, and occasionally a Pulitzer Prize winner or a professor at the local university cruises by and forces her to the floor and stuffs her skirt in her mouth, all the while babbling about freedom and responsibility and

how very much he admires strong, liberated, open-minded women.

Actually, girls have not only enjoyed all the hubbub and the ballyhoo of the past couple of decades, they have been meaning to write thank-you notes for all the help and all the well-meaning advice and all the attention. Like everyone else, girls have made a real effort to grasp the importance of pleasuring, sensate focus, pheromones, and G-spots, and they still like sex as much as they ever did. Indeed, so far as girls are concerned, promiscuity is a thinly sliced Italian cold cut and going all the way is the late movie in which Bing Crosby plays the priest. Girls believe that, where the average boy is concerned, statistics and theories are a lot less effective than footsie, Quaaludes, and slow dancing, and the willingness to listen to him, however long it takes, on how he couldn't possibly get into bed with her unless she first dressed up like a schoolmarm and beat him on the hamstrings with a pool cue. Girls in fact know more about the glory and the horror of sex than anyone; what girls suspect, though, is that the truth about sex can never be spoken, especially not to boys and certainly not to sex experts. They would never be able to take it.

HOW A GIRL KNOWS WHEN SHE'S GETTING HER PERIOD

She's ninety-nine percent certain that she's going to have to get out of bed and iron the creases out of her sheets.

She has eaten her way through two bags of Hershey's Kisses while waiting for the Milky Ways to freeze.

Whether the wineglass fell or she threw it, she couldn't exactly say.

It would be the most abandoned, passionate sex she's ever had, if only she had someone to have it with.

She knows for a fact that her phone is being tapped by the CIA.

The nearest all-night drugstore is two towns away.

If only none of the hairs on her head came anywhere near touching her face, she might stand a chance of living in peace.

She hasn't so much as kissed a boy in five weeks.

HOW A GIRL KNOWS WHEN SHE'S NOT GETTING HER PERIOD

She feels precisely the way she does the day before she gets her period.

Without provocation, her boyfriend delivers a soliloquy on how he can barely afford dinner for two anymore; and then, having paused for breath, he holds forth for the first time in months on his old fantasy of moving to Hawaii and trying to make a go of it as a nightclub comic.

Half an hour ago it was eight o'clock, it's eight o'clock now, and an hour from now it's still going to be eight o'clock.

She always comes up with exactly the same count.

Suddenly everything seems interconnected and fated.

Her boyfriend has broken down and begun asking her if she's gotten her period yet.

She tries to remember whether positive is good or negative is good.

Now she's really sure that she's getting her period.

WHAT GIRLS DO WHEN THEY'RE ALONE

Boys have two distinct theories about girls alone: one, that they temporarily cease to exist; two, that they dress in flannel pajamas with feet, preferably with kitten faces or little pink flowers on them, and curl up with a book, a hot water bottle, a cup of tea, *Dynasty*. The worst and most degraded of the boy theories is a sibling of the first: namely, that girls are never alone and if they claim they are alone, it means they are curled up with some other boy, probably a Hell's Angel.

Phone a girl on a Thursday evening and ask her what she's doing. If she says, "Oh, nothing really," she is likely to have gold glitter on her eyelids and a fuchsia mouth. She is seeing how her fake-fur, floor-length boa goes with her new fedora, sweat pants, and alligator spiked heels. She has piled the contents of her closet on her armchair. Her bank statement and last month's checks are spread out on her bed, beyond the take-out Chinese dinner. She is in the process of moving all her living room furniture into the bedroom and all the bedroom furniture into the living room. She has beef Bourguignon for twelve going on the stove and she's not expecting company. She is trying to figure out why her left speaker won't work. She is standing on her head.

Girls need time alone not for curling up but for catching up. Girls catch up with bills, laundry, dust, clogged pores, recipe editing, record album sorting, fall semester course selection. A girl catching up confronts a drawerful of letters with an eye to filing them neatly in a pastel accordion envelope with a little tie on the front. She rearranges all the shoes in her closet in order to free one shoe box for her swizzle stick collection. A girl catching

up is probably also a girl throwing out. She is attempting to part yet again with the plaid kilt she's had since ninth grade. She is wondering what the Salvation Army will actually *do* with the lime-green jumpsuit and what they'll think of her if she doesn't cut off the original price tag. A girl throwing out goes one on one with the past and always risks succumbing to it. She rereads her first boyfriend's bad poetry and falls asleep to *Bye, Bye, Birdie*.

A girl who does manage to catch up and throw out is ready for big plans—like Madame Curie in her Marja Sklodowska days, a Polish schoolgirl idly dreaming about one day falling in love with a nice guy and going on to give a name to radioactivity. A girl who wants to realize a vision begins by making lists. These come in two varieties: Action-Supply and Self-Improvement. The Action-Supply list is attached to the refrigerator with a magnet disguised as an insect or a vegetable. The Self-Improvement list is taped to the bathroom mirror at eye level. The list on the refrigerator says, "Buy birthday present for Suzanne. Buy Sara Lee chocolate cake." The list on the mirror says, "No cake this week!" and "Stick to budget—you can do it!" Some girls make lists the way other people take two aspirin and lie down for a few minutes. The lists are for temporary relief of anxiety. They are not necessarily consulted again.

The specific state of mind of a girl alone will always reflect her current relationship with a particular boy or with boys in general. A girl in between boyfriends is like Fred Lynn poised for a long pop fly to center field on a lazy August afternoon. He knows it's coming, nothing to do but be there, glove ready, smell the grass, wait for it, consider for the briefest of moments that fate is not always kind (maybe the ball will make an unaccountable left turn), think about dinner. Girls spending this kind of time alone think, "I will never have sex again." "I can't bear the thought of ever having sex again." "I've forgotten how to have sex." "What is sex?" Later, they stock up on contraceptive jelly and always have fresh sheets on the bed.

A girl recovering from a boy becomes her own private duty nurse. She lays on hands—on herself. Even in good times, her bed is command headquarters, communications center, dining room, lounge, fingernail clinic—she has even tried to iron on it. Now it becomes an intensive care unit. She plumps the pillows, throws on a comforter, moves the stereo nearby, cues up a this-man-is-gone record, and spends Saturday afternoon resting. She cuts toast on the diagonal and sprinkles cinnamon sugar on it. When she feels strong enough for solid food, she eats lamb chops, broccoli, and a baked potato. Though she's still quite weak, she makes chocolate pudding. She drags herself to the refrigerator for the white truffles she brought back from Italy and the bottle of champagne her mother's latest husband sent to butter her up. When two recovering girls call each other up and ask, "How are you?" they aren't being polite. They are taking each other's temperatures. "How are you?" is the girl theme song.

A girl alone because she is mad at a boy reads travel brochures on Morocco, gets out Living Language records to revive her French, and butters up her stepfather for air fare. She plots revenge fantasies featuring Mafia contracts, multiple Hell's Angels, and flagrante delicto. She slams a size twelve running shoe against the living room wall and makes a careful list of everything she thinks she left at his house. She telephones her five closest friends with intimate proof of male sexual insensitivity. Phone a girl who is mad at a boy and ask her what she's doing. She will tell you that just this minute she was finalizing plans to backpack in Thailand, join the Peace Corps, open a frozen yogurt stand in Paris—unless, that is, he has the common human decency to call.

THIRTEEN THINGS GIRLS WANT TO KEEP YOU IN THE DARK ABOUT

She has discovered that she actually has no trouble at all deciphering your personal correspondence if she holds the envelope up to a sunlamp.

Her teeth have another three years to go at an estimated cost of $8,250.

Despite what she said the other evening at dinner, she doesn't have the vaguest idea what the difference is between an IRA and a Keogh, and she honestly doesn't care either.

The same goes for further and farther.

Ditto imply and infer.

Once every two weeks, she goes to a downtown office building and rides an elevator to a salon where, for $40, she has the hair removed from her upper lip by a patented process called Forever-Off.

Her mother weighs 235 pounds and laughs like Tom Snyder.

The theme music from the telephone company's "Reach out and touch someone" commercials is alone enough to bring tears to her eyes.

Actually, she was three credits short of graduating.

She remembers which is right and which is left chiefly by virtue of wearing a cameo ring on the same side of her body on which she carries her handbag.

She thinks you're the nicest person she's ever met but, honestly, the sex was better with the guy she met on the Empress Line cruise in the Caribbean.

The way the phone rings sometimes and there's no one there when you pick it up? That's her checking to see if you're in or not, and whether you are or you aren't in, that's exactly the clue she was looking for.

The strange foreign-sounding person who kept calling your secretary to ask if it's true that Mr. So-and-so is really still out of town on business? That was her, too.

THE GIRL MIND

The girl mind is a complex system designed, according to guidelines from the League of Women's Voters, to provide high-quality government. The legislative branch of the girl mind is bicameral in organization: the pleasure center is on one side, the shopping center is on the other. The judiciary branch is staffed by nine no-nonsense nuns in leather habits and perfumed garter belts, a score of middle-aged ladies in pink and yellow dresses who organize tag sales and potluck suppers, or one Menachem Begin lookalike—depending. The chief executive is a Stanford MBA with a genius for unorthodox if-this-doesn't-work-out-you-can-reach-me-at-my-unlisted-number-in-Switzerland financing schemes; an enormous gusto for decision-making; no inhibitions about the 180 degree about-face; and a management philosophy that boils down to this: "See what you can do to pretty up the figures, then give it to PR and let them come up with a name for it." The executive also likes to take long vacations, during which the legislative and judiciary branches are left to batter each other about amid a welter of unresolved, and probably unresolvable, constitutional issues.

Topographically, the girl mind looks sort of like the sprawling exurban headquarters of a Fortune 500 corporation. Out on the lawn, there are pretty little gazebos, and at close, regular intervals amid the work spaces there are comfortable, well-equipped quiet rooms where a girl can go to get away from it all. In an out-of-the-way conference room, logic, judgment, and intuition argue the great questions of the day and jockey for the number one parking space. Behind a trompe l'oeil water cooler that is really

a door, a stairway leads to a small underground chamber where, among stuff a girl hasn't seen in years, an older man with graying temples and the evening newspaper beckons her to come and sit on his lap while a mean-looking witch, armed to the teeth with broomsticks and poisoned food, bars the way.

The memory center, next door to accounts receivable, is half-computerized, half a hopeless muddle of yellowing file cards, each detailing what someone ate, wore, and said on a particular evening in a particular restaurant, much of the information acquired at second or third hand; her brother's weak spots; the contents of her sister's diary; the multiplication tables except for the high ends of seven and eight; the number of calories in veal piccata; snapshots of a childhood summer at Cape Cod. Over a strongbox containing a lifetime of embarrassing moments, a chalkboard has been inscribed with the names of all the people she knows and, alongside the names, careful tick marks, cross-stroked after four, indicating the number of strikes they have against them.

Most of the time, the girl mind is a beehive of organized commotion. Operating at peak efficiency, it processes sensory data, rehearses comeback lines, puts together dinner parties, and periodically engages in a program of major long-range planning and reevaluation of the okay-now-what variety. Security in the girl mind is tight but not impenetrable, and sometimes a secret will leak out and some ignoble adversary will take advantage of it in order to wreak havoc. Then the girl mind is boggled or blown or, in extreme cases, shattered. The executive will rush back in from his Colorado mountain retreat. The pleasure center will temporarily lay off on the demands. Clerks in the memory center will go on overtime looking for instances of comparable behavior.

Sometimes an alien intruder will occupy so much space in the girl mind that there won't be enough room for both the alien and the girl, and then she has only two choices: Either she puts *it* out of her mind or she goes out of her mind herself, and she probably would go out of her mind from time to time if only she were confident that they had clean sheets there. In the very worst situations, a girl may think that she is positively losing her mind or that she is actually being driven out of her mind, though when this happens she will normally ask to be dropped at the airport so that she can catch the first plane to Barbados, where she has found in the past that she gets along very nicely without it.

HOW GIRLS EVALUATE EVIDENCE

In the universe that girls inhabit, nothing happens casually, nothing is as it seems—indeed, every road, every byway is strewn with misleading clues and double meanings.

A girl thinks, "The phone rang twenty times. That means he must be in."

"He looked really happy to see me. He must have met someone else."

"He forgot to take his scarf. There's a message in that."

Though girls lack formal training in the forensic sciences of fingerprint dusting, chemical analysis, and polygraph; although they work for the most part without dogs, they are first-class sleuths. They make do with the tools at hand—the eavesdrop, the grapevine, Standard & Poors, the telephone directory, the designer label, the stakeout. A girl wants to know: *Who is he? Who is he really? What are his intentions? How many nights a week can he actually take a creative writing course?* No matter what her particular prejudice of the moment, a girl, like a smart DA, can always find evidence to support it. The difference between the girl and the DA is that the girl imagines there really *is* a truth somewhere. As it happens, every case she actually works on turns out to be like one of those tricky modern stage plays in which the person under surveillance has as little idea of the truth as the girl who wants to uncover it.

THE SPECIAL MEANING OF CUTENESS IN THE MENTAL LIFE OF GIRLS

When people in general mean to express their highest esteem, they call upon words such as excellent, peerless, superb, splendid, A-OK, and tops. When girls mean to express their highest praise, they call upon the word *cute*—though, since the word has become somewhat threadbare, hardly anything is just cute anymore; rather it is really cute, incredibly cute, unbelievably cute or, at the high end of the scale, sweet. Girls recognize cuteness in Cabbage Patch dolls, baby coyotes, patent leather pumps, boys who went to Dartmouth, the look on the Elephant Man's face when Anne Bancroft reads *Romeo and Juliet* to him, the works of Franz Kafka. When a girl says something is cute, what she really means is that she'd like to take it home with her and talk to it under the covers. When a girl wants to demonstrate that she is moved not simply by the force of her emotions but is exercising critical judgment, she trots out adorable, precious, or darling.

GIRLS AND THE WEATHER

Cut off as she is from agriculture, knowing nothing about the food chain other than that the A&P owns several stores in her town, a girl would just as soon the weather be clement all the time—except when the monotony gets to her or else her own inner weather is so turbulent that she craves a good strong pathetic fallacy, the same as in *Breakfast at Tiffany's* when Holly Golightly has the mean reds and everything's a mess and all of a sudden the sky opens up and starts pouring on her. When a girl is in high spirits and the weather has a mind of its own, a girl poses a few simple questions: Can she make it from her apartment to the bus without an umbrella, or should she walk back up the three flights of stairs and take a chance on being late? Supposing she doesn't go back, what confidence can she have that her office umbrella *is* in her office and not dangling from the counter of the coffee shop where she ate lunch the last time it didn't rain? Should she just call in sick and start fresh tomorrow? While a girl is waiting for Johnny Carson to come on, it would, accordingly, not displease her if the weatherman laid off the isobars and the high systems and the fronts moving down from Canada and simply told her what the goddamn weather was going to be, and how long it was going to last.

GIRLS AND GOD

Despite all of the past decade's considerable enthusiasm for Ishtar, Isis, and Rhea, girls have not entirely given up on the idea that God is a guy. He is not, on the other hand, a guy they have very much interest in dating. Girls by and large believe in God on a just-in-case, you-never-know basis—kind of the way they pack a diaphragm when they go to the movies. On Sundays girls like to sleep late, and from Monday through Saturday girl appetite for the supernatural is pretty much satisfied by the horoscope. When girls wonder about what happens after you die, the questions that bother them the most are: Will Anita feel bad that Pam got the fur, and will Judy remember not to tell Laurie how she happens to own a queen-size down comforter?

GIRLS AND THE OCCULT

It is often said that the secrets of the universe are revealed on a need-to-know basis, and this is why a girl believes that palm readers and clairvoyants and the connect-the-dots horoscopes on diner placemats are likely to have important messages for her—nobody needs to know more than she does. Girls live in a universe of signs and portents. If the bus driver smiles at a girl in the morning and the coffee wagon lady hasn't run out of Drake's cakes and the quarter in change comes up heads, then she'll be rich and famous within the year, and if it doesn't come up heads it's two out of three. When a girl gives up a lunch hour at the health club and buses across town to consult a psychic who has not only located missing persons for seven New Jersey police departments but eligible males for her three best friends, she is in fact only superficially different from the Stone Age savage who grabbed a cloak and a torch and hiked off to consult a similar professional halfway across Easter Island: The savage spun around three times and sacrificed a chicken, the modern girl practices automatic check writing.

The way boys see it, the average psychic is unlikely to know much more about the future than tomorrow's four o'clock movie. Girls are convinced that the future is either knowable or it is not knowable, and if it is knowable it is no more astonishing that it should be disclosed by an astral body speaking through Shirley MacLaine than by John Kenneth Galbraith or Milton Friedman. Girls are inclined to believe that all the forces of the cosmos work together to insure that when two people meet for dinner at a Chinese restaurant, each picks up his or her specifically preordained fortune cookie. Girls are undecided on the efficacy of voodoo, the idea that by sticking a pin into a rag doll in a bedroom in Santa Monica they can cause convulsions three thousand miles away in the office of a Wall Street stockbroker. But they are looking into it.

GIRLS AND HISTORY

Eve didn't do it, the snake did. Then men fought a whole bunch of wars, mostly about religion and things. Of course, the Greeks were all gay, kind of waterfront types. This is why they fought so well together. *This is no secret.* Supposedly it's all in Plato. The women were used for breeding. Forget it. Then a bunch of men got together and stabbed Caesar outside the Forum, or

B.C. | | | | | | | A.D. | | | | | | | | 7 p.m.
June

maybe it was outside the Senate, and Caesar said, "Et tu, Brute?" *Caesar was not faithful to his wife*. But don't blame Cleopatra. She was just looking out for her own interests. So she used a little feminine guile. So what? Caesar was deaf and bald. He was no catch. And Antony was just a sexed-up power freak. Then for a long time nothing happened, except even less happened for women, and in every way their condition was worse. Catherine the Great came along at some point in here. She was kind of a black widow spider—wait, that might have been Elizabeth I. Anyway, they say that Catherine died trying to have sex with her horse. Some people say she didn't. Nobody knows. Josephine was all right—the one who married Napoleon. He was always traveling around a lot, sleeping with foreign girls, because of his height. At least Josephine didn't sit home and worry about it. She had lovers, too. Nicholas and Alexandra were so sad, especially that scene in the movie just before the execution where they say their last good-bye. Marie Antoinette was real community college material. Talk about princesses. There *are* witches, but they're good, not bad. Then in the Victorian period women never had orgasms; they weren't even supposed to move around when they had sex, and the men were very stuffy and smelled like cigars. Basically, there was repression.

For girls, all history essentially happens in the present or, more precisely, at one crowded moment in the past just before the assassination of John Kennedy, the Watergate hearings, or the Iranian hostage crisis, depending on any particular girl's chronological age.

GIRLS AND NUMBER

Girls like numbers for their ethical and emotive value, their connotative expressiveness—not for their specificity.

Girls, consequently, round off a lot, usually to the nearest zillion.

When a girl says a million zillion, she has in mind something like the number of people that turn up at Times Square on New Year's Eve—or around Saks Fifth Avenue's glove counter for the Labor Day sale.

When a girl says trillions, she means roughly ninety.

When a girl says millions, she means—give or take—forty.

When a girl says thousands, she means three or four.

When a girl says one or two or a couple, as in a couple of chocolates, one drink, or one kiss, by contrast, she normally means a baker's dozen or eight.

I-can't-tell-you-how-many is the general term for the kind of large number, approaching infinity, that physicists and mathematicians represent by high-order exponents. Umpteen, scads, and the daringly unabashed "oodles and oodles" are synonyms of I-can't-tell-you-how-many, though they are rarely encountered anymore outside of country clubs and suburban real estate sales offices. Another synonym, the prim and heartrending one-hundred-and-one, survives chiefly among students of Early Childhood Education.

Mel Brooks's two thousand-year-old man is definitely (a girl word) a male concept. If a girl had been in the driver's seat, the guy would have been an easy hundred thousand even before he had I-can't-tell-you-how-many candles on his birthday cake.

THE GIRL GOSPEL OF PEACE THROUGH MUTUAL UNDERSTANDING

Girls believe that the world would be a safer and more secure place to bring up future generations if only leaders would get to know each other better and talk more. This would mean their not just having a hot line but using it, kind of like an open wire, so that whenever they weren't doing something else, like having meetings with commissars or cabinet ministers about important local issues, they would talk on it. Just talk. Maybe half an hour every day after dinner minimum. Where did you go to high school? Where did I go to high school? Do we know any of the same people? That sort of thing. And they should talk about their feelings more.

They should not talk about world affairs necessarily. This is one of the places they go wrong now. When they get onto world affairs, they get on each other's nerves, so they should talk about other things and then occasionally slip in a little world affairs talk, and if it doesn't go over well, then they should back off and

not push it too much, and instead talk more about their favorite restaurants and who they know in common and the weather. They should keep coming back to world affairs and trying to make progress, but they shouldn't get each other's dander up.

Girls also believe that anyone who expects to be a world leader should study other languages in college and at least make an effort—so what if they're not sure of the subjunctive or they don't roll the *r*'s just right? That's not what starts wars, and people are flattered that you at least try. Just a simple *bon jour* or a *da* or a *nyet* might actually help a lot. Make people smile.

World leaders should also eat each other's foods; the Americans should learn about blinis and caviar and shrimp in lobster sauce and shish kebab, and the Russians should learn about Texas Bar-B-Q and so forth, and everyone should always be complimentary. If you don't like the basic meat, like if you're not accustomed to eating monkey, then say something nice about the sauce, and if you can't think of anything nice to say, don't say anything. We're all human beings underneath.

These are girls' true views on the international mess, but in order to get this kind of thing out of them you either have to keep them up very late, preferably into the idealistic wee hours, or else get them going on Mai-Tais. Over a sober business lunch, they're capable of the same blood-curdling cut-the-bastards-up-and-unleash-the-Rapid-Deployment-Force-on-them that you can get from anyone else.

SEVENTEEN GIRL FEARS, EACH MORE POTENTIALLY DEVASTATING THAN NUCLEAR HOLOCAUST

Saying yes

Saying no

Dry skin

That the therapist will tell her she's better and she doesn't have to come anymore

That by the time she gets happy she won't have a body to enjoy it with

Living alone and getting to like it

That she'll never have sex again

That she *will* have sex again and it will be awful

Winding up a childless bag lady

The discontinuance of Tender Moonlight Blush

New Year's Eve with a blind date

Being stood up

That if she doesn't carry a sweater she may be a little chilly

That mother was wrong

That mother was right

What he'll think of her in the morning

Senseless, incomprehensible abandonment

GIRLS AND THE OFFICE

Each weekday morning a girl will put up with gridlocked traffic and cardboard coffee cake and painfully inane elevator talk in order to move her base of operations to an office—ideally, one with unmonitored direct long-distance dialing privileges, an incoming line for each of her five best friends, someone to fill out pink IMPORTANT MESSAGE slips for her when she goes out shopping, all the nondairy creamer a human being could ask for, profit sharing, a place to change before dinner and the theater, the court-guaranteed right to be treated as if her sex were a matter of utter indifference—plus, if she's lucky, a title she can wear,

as is, to her high school reunion. Whereas when a boy is hired he joins a team, searches out a safe spot to stash his *Penthouses*, and positions his wastebasket to receive hook shots, a newly hired girl establishes her place in a family and decorates her work space in imitation of the bedroom she occupied in her parents' house during her cheerleader days. She brings in the cat calendars, the vases, the heating elements, the bouillon cubes, the Wheat Thins, the zodiac coffee mugs. She covers a bulletin board with a whole relationship's worth of Chinese cookie fortunes and a half-dozen funny sayings of her own, assembled, in the manner

of a kidnapper's ransom note, out of unrelated newspaper head-lines. She hangs a Richard Gere poster over where the last girl wrecked the wall with a knickknack shelf.

A boy in an office situation engages in competitive scrambles; a girl, in sibling rivalries—with two or three sisters who think they can triumph over her by making her look bad and a still-greater number of brothers, most of them on second warning most of the time, who think they can get by on their charm and good looks. In addition to siblings, a girl's office family consists of three or four idiot uncles, a couple of alcoholic uncles, one who would probably be in jail if the family didn't believe in keep-ing its dirty laundry private, a mother who acts as if the future of the free world rested on her guardianship of the supply cabinet, a couple of aunts whose real job seems to be birthday party catering, half a dozen cousins who can't decide whether they're gay or not, a father who's away on business trips so often that the aunts wonder about calling security when they see him prowl-ing around, and a drug connection in the mail room.

Because girls have so many nonbusiness activities to see to, many people have the idea that girls don't work hard. This is a big mistake. Girls don't just work hard, they work efficiently. And in this respect the state-of-the-art working girl is as big an improvement over boys as a computer is over a roomful of un-imaginative accountants. A girl can wake up in some date's barely recognizable bedroom, and go on to triumph over the worst sorts of adversity imaginable. She will make do with an inferior and perhaps disease-carrying washcloth, a sliver of bad soap, detergent-strength shampoo, and a toothpaste that can only have turned up free in the mailbox. She will use the hair conditioner as moisturizer and make up her entire face with one tube of lipstick.

She will make a thousand decisions along the way: Should she wash her hair and, if so, how will she dry it? Does she even want to shower in such a place? Suppose she appears before him in wet hair, what will he think? Will he be contemptuous of her if she takes more than seven minutes to get up, get bathed, and get out? She will already have spent the early part of the morning wondering if she should put more stuff in her diaphragm—and looking forward to what the office mother will say about her turning up in the same clothes for two days running. She will, moreover, do all of this for a guy who, in three months, is going to make a speech beginning, "Now, don't take this personally," then drift into the familiar waters of, "Well, I don't know, I guess I'd like to spend some time alone"—whose whole philosophy of business, in any case, is that just showing up is fifty percent and the other fifty percent is remembering enough about last night's football game or *Hill Street Blues* to make the proper sounds in the company of the other guys. And, in spite of all this, she will have figured out where to take the new client for lunch, written and edited a sales report in her head, calculated the profit in another hundred unit sales to the Mexican government, had a major revelation of how one of her five best friends could improve *her* business by turning the basement into retail space —plus she has come a couple of steps closer to rounding out her own plan to resign in three years and open up a shop of her own.

GIRLS AND THE CHAIN OF COMMAND

If girls were ever really put in charge of things, pyramidal organization charts would probably be redesigned as circles and no
one would ever leave a meeting without thinking that it had been
an extremely positive experience and that now everyone was
definitely going to work together. No one would ever really be
fired either, they'd just take hints; then they'd slink off quietly,
maybe leaving a note about how "This is all for the best" and
"long overdue" and "Thanks for the help and encouragement."
Girls are considerably less exhilarated than boys at the thought
of giving orders to people to whom they are not related by blood
or marriage. Nevertheless, girls sometimes enjoy giving orders,
and they are always pleasantly surprised when someone actually
carries them out. Girls are also pleasantly surprised that, if you
explain things slowly and patiently to male subordinates, they
usually get at least the major points and, if you take them to
lunch once in a while and listen to their problems, they do ac-
ceptable work without a lot of supervision. Girls think that someday it might be nice to be president of something and fly around
in a private plane. They also think that, for the time being, the
title vice-president has a nice authority about it. Indeed, if girls
used to dream about being executive secretary and marrying the
boss, now they mostly dream about being vice-president for stra-
tegic planning and marrying their mentor. Girls know that having
a carpet on the floor means something or other to men about
power; girls just like carpets.

GIRLS IN GROUPS

"Did you see that?"

"See what?"

"It just walked through the door—looked like some huge furry thing."

"Bunch of girls."

"Huh?"

"Girls. They come in here sometimes, a lot of them together. You know, after work."

"What is it, choir practice or something?"

"Nah, it's like the beach, only dressed and standing up."

"You sure it's not a movement? It's definitely moving this way."

"They're going to the bathroom. Then they come out, sort of splinter off, get glued back up when it's time to go."

GIRLS AND FOOD

The entire girl experience of what used to be thought of as the moral life—namely, resistance to temptation—is now lived out almost exclusively in relation to food. The reason for this is that, though girls know food can be a valuable source of roughage and fiber, they also know it as a fool's paradise of empty calories and cheap highs and hence as the shortest possible route to obesity and an endless string of Saturday night dates with Ricardo Montalban. Generally speaking, it is a girl's strategy not to eat at all or, if she must eat, to confine herself to pencil ends, eyeglass stems, candle wax, straws, and an occasional leaf of macrobiotic lettuce. Because a girl does not entirely trust herself, however, she will set up an elaborate control system of bathroom scales, calorie counters, fitness programs, full-length mirrors, prescription drugs, and a fabulous spandex and leather wardrobe that she doesn't have a prayer of packing herself into unless she loses another seven pounds. Indeed, even in a pitch-black movie theater where a girl goes to pig out in peace and quiet, she will load up not just on Raisinets but on Jujyfruits, on the certain knowledge that she would sooner starve to death than eat the yellows or the greens.

When a girl is alone at home in the evening, she owes her survival to self-delusion and the enormous pleasure she takes in her good intentions. A girl does not say to herself, "I think I shall stand over the sink with the refrigerator door open and eat some twenty-five or thirty stoned wheat crackers, maybe half with peanut butter and the other half with onion dip and horseradish, then I shall assemble all of the necessary ingredients for brownies." She does not say, "I shall demonstrate the possibility of sustaining life without washing a plate or turning on a flame." She says, "I think I shall make myself a nice little piece of Dover sole and I shall set myself a place at the table and I shall pour a glass of wine and I shall treat myself with the respect and courtesy due a human being." A girl, however, will not only exhaust her interest in the Dover sole by shopping for it, she will experience such intense futility and ennui that she will abandon her shopping cart mid-aisle and hope that she can make it to the door without running into the manager and having to give up her courtesy card. When a girl accepts an invitation to have dinner with a boy in a restaurant, she is always on her very best behavior and she always orders a compromise between the king crab appetizer and sixteen-ounce sirloin she really wants and the cheddar cheeseburger and french fries she suspects he is likely to pay for ungrudgingly. She also tries to remember to chew before swallowing, and she does not presume to pick at the scraps and wastage on his plate until at least the third date.

A girl's refrigerator—part museum and part morgue—usually contains several French mustards that are too full to throw out and too old to risk eating, several tinfoil sculptures housing unidentifiable chicken parts that are too far gone even to touch, and a freezer full of ice cream. The ideal girl food is portable and user-friendly and it comes in numerous small units—cherries, grapes, mixed nuts, popcorn, Cheez-Its, Pepperidge Farm Lidos. With any of these edibles a girl can convince herself that she's about to close the container and safeguard at least some small part of the pleasure for breakfast. In fact, any such meal is open-ended, and a girl knows it is over only when her stomach threatens to go over her head and call for an ambulance.

GIRLS AND DRINK

To make a girl's drink, you begin by omitting the scotch and the bourbon, which a few adult women like but no girl likes. What does go into a girl drink is a mystery to everyone except professional bartenders. Girls know that they like rum and that they like pineapple juice; they know that they like straws, parasols, and crushed ice. They have a vague intuition that somewhere along the line the sugar content of a Snickers bar gets poured in. But, beyond that, a piña colada or a Singapore sling is, for all a girl knows, as much a basic building block of the universe as cadmium or lithium. Girls have also not noticed that when they have a hankering for one of these drinks, boys don't order until they've looked around to make sure that none of their friends are watching. If girls have ever noticed that boys drink scotch and men, bourbon, they have never said anything about it.

Girls always mean to drink eight glasses of water a day, because water is well known to have beneficial effects on both the

complexion and the kidneys. Instead they drink wine, because wine has a beneficial effect on conversation and, besides, unlike a decent glass of water, you can get it almost anywhere and it doesn't make you gag. Whatever the truth may be about boys, girls are not born with a taste for beer, nor do they have any instinctual sense that the keg is the natural unit of liquid measure. Girls do, however, drink beer with their sushi and with their enchiladas and refried beans, just as long as no boy tries to convince them that it's possible to celebrate anything with it.

Girls do not experiment with drinks much. They meet one they like and they go to the altar with it, particularly if it has the kind of dangerous-sounding name that would look right on the card for Georgia Championship Wrestling: the zombie, the stinger, the earthquake, the Black Russian, the Harvey Wallbanger.

Girl drinking habits are so different from boy drinking habits that most boys wonder if girls even like drinking. They do, they do, provided the taste of the liquor is disguised and they don't wind up vomiting their guts out in a tavern toilet at closing time. Girls have a lower tolerance for vomiting than boys do. It also takes a lot less to get them going. A girl knows that when a boy invites her out for a drink for the first time, he always has it in the back of his head to get her a little tipsy and then have some real fun with her in the back of something or other, just as if it were still 1957 and real life imitated *Animal House* or *Porky's II*. Girls think that they can take care of themselves. Girls believe that drink is sinful—not the way sex is but the way banana splits are—and considering what it is they drink they're not so far from the truth.

GIRLS AND OTHER PEOPLE'S WEDDINGS

To begin with, girls like other people's weddings for being the closest that they will ever come to attending in person the coronation of an English monarch. If the whole thing is pulled off with any panache, a girl gets ritual, she gets ceremony, she gets consecutive and sometimes overlapping rushes of happiness and sadness, she gets the "Wedding March," pale colors, melon balls, slow dancing, a couple of drunken flirtations, and the unshakable conviction that she is destined to meet a perfect, cute boy from the other side of the aisle. At the same time, a girl gets to exercise her acute taste and dazzling judgment as social critic and observer. Was the seating of the people in the far corner of the tent deliberate? Is there anyone in the party so appalling that *all* second cousins should have been excluded? Are they somehow going to be able to gloss up her last three marriages and his junior college so that it all looks okay in the newspaper? Girls think that elopements are romantic enough and make good stories afterward, but people also have some kind of obligation to the community as a whole, don't they?

HOW GIRLS THINK ABOUT MARRIAGE

It's the same as living together, except you get to move him into the smaller closet and you can start taking the mascara off before you go to sleep and also you get a little more time to yourself.

Supposedly they treat you with a little more respect in the shops.

The sex gets better for a while, then worse, then something incredible happens when you get really old. It's hard to remember exactly what, but there are articles about it in *McCall's*.

Look at Steve and Eydie.

If a marriage is any good, you eat out in restaurants most of the time.

As long as part of you wants to kill the other person, you know that everything's okay.

Tom Hayden and Jane Fonda talk about issues.

These days when you check into a hotel or a motel nobody even bats an eyelash, so what conceivable difference does it make?

If his record albums and her record albums are kept in separate boxes, it's not necessarily such a bad idea, and sometimes it saves an awful lot of rancor and discord later on.

If it doesn't work out, there's always Larry.

If your parents told you to jump off the Brooklyn Bridge, you wouldn't do that, would you?

People don't fool around much with the marriage ceremony anymore; it's the language in the lease that matters.

All marriages are basically power relationships. They proved that in the mid-seventies.

Look at *A Doll's House*.

Omnia vincit amor.

Look at the Samoans.

HOW GIRLS VACATION

A girl doesn't really start a vacation until she's already had the first complimentary cocktail and all her hopefulness and all her nervous excitement come up against the grim actuality of a particular room in a particular vacation village on a particular island, probably in the Caribbean, and she realizes that she never wanted to go away in the first place. It wasn't even her idea, it was her mother, her sister, her best friend, not least of all her travel agent telling her that it would be good for her; she can feel the plants in her living room window withering, the junkies rifling her jewelry box, she hasn't seen a single cute boy—and she bursts into tears. The next night she wears the off-the-shoulder dress, and the night after that she seriously considers not going back at all and just having them airmail the cat, care of American Express.

A girl is always torn between going someplace that is improving because it has ancient ruins and culture and the natives speak

a language she studied in high school and just going someplace hot but not too humid where they mass-produce suntans and let you samba all night. A girl would want to go to the improving places and probably like looking at paintings, too, if only she could get over the feeling of here-I-am-looking-at-paintings. The best vacation a girl ever had was the time she traveled through France and Italy with her boyfriend and stayed in charming country inns and had a hair dryer that could actually be made to work, and one afternoon at lunch outside of Lyons she thought she had transcended herself, but you had to be there. The worst vacation a girl ever had was the time she went to Norway with her mother and cruised the fjords and was seated at dinner with a dentist and his wife from St. Louis. When a girl comes back from vacation, she knows for a fact that Jackie Onassis was once secretly married to Dick Cavett because she just happens to have stayed up half the night with a masseuse who got it from David Susskind.

GIRLS AND THEIR FRIENDS, PART I

All girls have two friends. Their names are Scylla and Charybdis.

GIRLS AND THEIR FRIENDS, PART II

Scylla is attractive in a severe way, Charybdis is cute and verging on the flirtatious. Boys are advised to keep hands off, because both retain fingerprints like the handle of a Browning automatic. Passion tells girls that they can get along without their friends better than they can get along without boys. Reason tells them that they can get along without boys better than they can get along without their friends.

WHAT GIRLS TALK ABOUT THE MORNING AFTER THE DATE

"Hi. Are you alone?"

"He just left."

"Did you have breakfast in or out?"

"In. Can I ask you a question?"

"Go ahead."

"Tell me what you think this means. When he left, he didn't say, 'I'll call you,' which I wouldn't have been able to stand, it would have seemed so distant, like 'Let's have lunch sometime.' He said, 'That was the best coffee I ever had.' Do you think that's a good sign?"

"How was the sex?"

"We did it three times. God, it was incredible. He's a wonderful kisser. I mean, it wasn't the most passionate sex I've ever had, but very nice. Tender. Maybe we did it only twice. Once was in the middle of the night—that part's a little hazy. He kept whispering things to me I couldn't exactly hear. Do you think that's a lot of sex or not enough?"

"It depends what you consider a night, whether it was from eight-thirty till three in the morning or eleven-thirty till nine. It depends."

"He's very, very cute. Kind of Robert De Niro but without the swagger. And we think exactly alike. He likes the same music I do, and he hates people who walk their children on a leash. And listen to this: He brought me a seashell. Isn't that adorable? And he laughed at all my jokes. I suppose the sex will get better."

"When are you going to see him again?"

"God, I don't know. I wish he'd said something about calling.

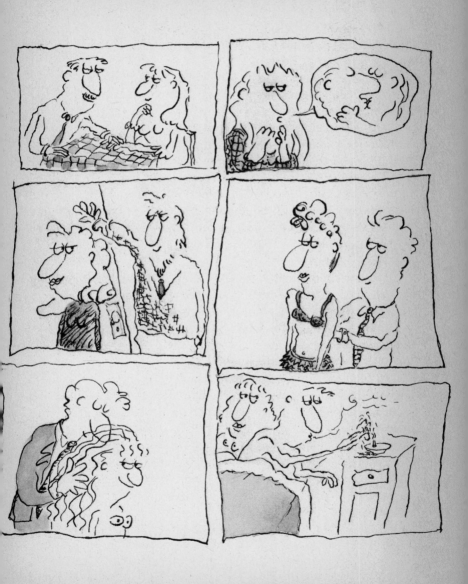

He didn't say anything about calling. I'm not going to call him. If only I'd heard what he kept whispering to me, but he sort of had his elbow over my ear. I shouldn't call him, should I? If he wanted to see me again, wouldn't he have said something more definite? Maybe I could call him just to say hello.''

"He'll call. If he doesn't, he's a jerk.''

"You know what I really like about him? He's so different from me. He told me this story about a videotape he made in college, for his senior thesis or something. The whole thing consisted of two old people sitting on a park bench and a pigeon kind of pecking around them. He was really proud of it. I mean, I didn't get the point exactly. The film itself sounded kind of boring.''

"Did he ask you a lot of questions about yourself?''

"Mmmm . . . what? I'm sorry, I was just remembering something. Did I say what he was wearing? Blue jeans. And a sweater. Kind of ratty. But, you know, perfect.''

"What did you do?''

"We had dinner at this sort of divey place where everybody looked, I don't know, interesting. He touched me on the hand a lot; you know, while we were talking? And he had this nice way with the waiter—confident, but not condescending or anything. Actually, I think he's basically a very shy person.''

"Want to meet at the health club later?''

"Or he could be a jerk. I don't know. I don't think so. I guess I'll just have to wait and see. But don't you think it would have been more polite if he'd said something about getting together again?''

"Yeah, he should have. Robert De Niro swaggers?''

FIFTEEN THINGS EVERY GIRL'S BEST FRIEND TELLS HER

"If he loves you very much and just can't show it, get rid of him."

"All it takes is one good man."

"All the good men are taken."

"There are no good men."

"It's not you he doesn't like, it's himself."

"You used to have a better sense of humor."

"It will grow out."

"Are you kidding? You're much prettier than she is."

"You look great. I look terrible."

"You look terrible."

"I promise not to tell."

"Don't go. You're not going to marry him."

"Sometimes you can analyze things too much."

"If only you were a man I'd marry you."

"You can always return it."

BAD GIRLS GOOD GIRLS ENVY

Evita

Rebecca

Lolita

Oriana Fallaci

Princess Margaret

Margaret Trudeau

Tina Turner

Cher

Abby Ewing

Mae West

GOOD GIRLS BAD GIRLS WISH THEY WERE MORE LIKE

Anne Frank

Annie

Mrs. Roosevelt

Loretta Lynn

Mother Teresa

THE THREE WAYS GIRLS GO SHOPPING

I

When a girl's immune system is in tiptop shape, she can sail into a department store and shop the merchandise without having any of it follow her back onto the street. If a salesperson asks her, "Can I help you?" she will say, "No thank you, I'm just looking"; and if a salesperson tells her what a big mistake she would be making if she didn't at least try on the new red coatdress, she will be deaf to the siren song. A girl with her immunity up might have $500 cash in her pocket and a clean credit card, and all she will do is finger a few hems, inquire about size and color availability, and still just not feel like getting undressed.

II

On other occasions, a girl sails into a department store and she knows she's going to buy exactly what she wants to buy and nothing that she doesn't want to buy. She might have them

shorten it. She might get it in plum instead. She might take it with her. She might have it sent. But, whatever she does, it's going to be a pleasurable experience, and several days later when she takes off the price tags and wears it for the first time, it's still going to be a pleasurable experience and she may even feel a little bit smug, as if it were a deal to produce the definitive movie version of the phone directory that she had put together and not just a skirt and a blouse.

III

Sometimes when a girl goes shopping, she has a bad spirit in her. She knows one thing absolutely: She cannot afford to be in this store. Nevertheless, there she is, breezing through the revolving doors, huge waves of anxiety and greed and guilt driving her across the main floor, images of the late notices on top of the bill she already can't pay warning her away from cosmetics, where

one tube of lipstick is bound to lead to an entire skin care program and financial ruin. The driven shopping girl with the bad spirit in her goes straight to three—Designer. She knows that she is about to cause damage and that it is the kind of damage that has nothing to do with will and even less with taste. Within the past twenty-four hours it has become obvious to her that nothing in her wardrobe can ever be worn again. Here, everything looks good, or nothing does; it doesn't matter, it's impossible to know, at least it doesn't make her sick.

Of course, even as she loads down the salesperson with alternate sizes, some with stitched-down pleats, some that button down the back, in some dim part of her mind she has already begun to think, "Return." It is as if an emergency relief center is being set up to handle this mess, as if the disease has progressed so far that the organism has begun automatically to fight back, and the worst hasn't even happened yet. In the dressing room, the fevered shopping girl abandons all hope of simply walking out empty-handed and gives herself over to the rest of the performance. She will encourage another customer to buy the loden-green cashmere cape sweater. She will offer an appraisal of the weather. She will produce the two pieces of identification. As they wrap it all up, she throws in a gratuitous "I know I'll love it" or "I'm so glad I happened in" and maybe she throws in an accessory. Out on the street, the performance over, she drags the shopping bag behind her like a crabby, overtired child. Much to her astonishment, no one arrests her.

GIRLS AND MONEY IN GENERAL

Because girls neither earn a lot of money nor inherit it nor even do well on average with lottery tickets or the Publishers Clearing House, their principal experience of money is having to come up with it, usually at short notice and usually in multiples of $5,000. Girls get into fixes because, like financiers, they live at the edge of a precipice. A girl's ability to take cabs and buy good soaps and overtip porters is a measure only of the cash she has in her pockets, and that in turn is a measure only of her having remembered to borrow a twenty from the cleaning lady, not of her overall solvency. A girl is in fact always weighing her stack of unopened bills against an up-to-date mental inventory of her negotiable liquid assets: her grandmother's emerald and ruby earrings, the upright piano she never plays on any more, her original Ink Spots records, John Irving's warm response to her fan letter, her college textbooks, her own charms. A girl also regularly reviews her portfolio of push-come-to-shove financial procedures: transferring, mortgaging, cashing in, disconnecting her telephone, hiding under the covers, marrying the sporting goods mogul from Utica. Fortunately, when a girl has to come up with $5,000, all she really needs is $350. With $5,000, she could make everything perfect. For $350, she can hold everyone at bay for another month.

GIRLS AND THE BALANCE OF PAYMENTS

If inside every woman there is a girl, inside every girl there is a grande dame waiting to get out at the eighth-floor credit department. The grande dame is a puffed-up creature of last-ditch hauteur and fragile indignation, and her basic point of view on things is that there has apparently been some mistake. Whereas the girl would be satisfied with saying, "Just because I do not have the money to pay my bill does not mean that I am not a fine person from a good home," the grande dame delivers a speech based on what she dimly remembers her mother and Bette Davis to have said in comparable situations: "If Bergdorf Goodman can have the grace to allow me to settle my account over a period of six months, what right does Bloomingdale's have to insist on every last drop of my blood?" The girl, with her deep-down conviction that finances should be juggled in the privacy of one's own bedroom, takes a certain umbrage at having to write a bad check in public. The grande dame, who thinks that even a bad check is too good for these people, takes names and demands photocopies of her last year's bills in hopes of finding the $1.50 mistake that will vindicate her. The girl and her grande dame finally come as close to flouncing out as is humanly possible in a brand new Anne Klein side-snapped mini-dress, itself a contributor to the present predicament, and they pause only at the main floor cosmetics counter to charge a new lipstick and blusher.

GIRLS AND FOREIGN MONEY

Next to explaining to the shopkeeper that, no, she's not a native but only visiting, it is the successful manipulation of a foreign currency that gives the girl traveler her most intense feeling of mastery. No girl has ever changed dollars into francs at Charles De Gaulle Airport without experiencing a dizzying rush of power, and this is true even if she has changed only a twenty-dollar traveler's check to tide her over until she can find a more favorable rate on another thirty dollars. Girls approach foreign money studiously. While the people sharing her compartment on a long train trip are reading crime thrillers, a girl is reading her currency and trying to figure out if *perpétuité* means the same thing as forever, or something else. Girls tend to accumulate vast quantities of coin because they always pay for their purchases with a fresh bill, usually their largest, except at the end of a hot afternoon when they abandon pride, extend to a shopkeeper all the bills in their possession, and let him take what he likes. When a girl returns home, American money looks colorless and unappealing, and it continues to look colorless and unappealing throughout the entire cab ride home from the airport. For the next month or so, a girl will nevertheless always carry on her person her last ten franc note, along with her passport, on the theory that, you never know, you might have to go back on short notice. Years later, she finds the bank note marking her place near the beginning of the first volume of Proust.

GIRLS AND CARS

When a girl gets a new car, the first thing she does is set the buttons on the radio and move in; she moves in the you-can-overcome-sales-resistance cassettes, the Kleenex, the sunglasses, the pillow, the blanket, the umbrella, the sweater, the extra sneakers, and several emergency restaurant packs of Sweet 'N Low. When a girl and her car get on speaking terms with each other, she also gives it a name—maybe something like Mighty Mo if she thinks of it as a powerhouse, Jezebel if whenever she runs the air conditioner and the radio at the same time it pulls over to the side of the road and knocks off for the afternoon. In relation to cars, girls differ from boys in the following respects. When a boy can't start an uncooperative car, his instinct is to open the hood and shake his head; a girl's instinct is to talk to the thing pleadingly: "Come on, baby, you can do it if you try. Mama has confidence." This large difference in strategy reflects a still-larger difference in philosophy: Boys think that any electromechanical object is fundamentally sound as long as the motor

can be made to hum; girls are satisfied if the plastic casing doesn't have any cracks in it and the guys at the minute wash continue to sell her high quality sinsemilla.

Boys with their great derring-do and unshakable faith in their own infallible sense of direction believe that girls get lost more often than boys do; in fact, girls just admit to being lost more often and are less embarrassed to ask for directions. Boys, with their undying faith in the possibility of perpetual motion, also believe that girls are worrywarts about gas levels and that, if a girl says she needs to stop to go to the bathroom, she is in fact trying to trick him into filling up the tank without forcing him to admit he's wrong. Girls, in any case, are right that when the needle shows empty and a boy claims he has enough fuel to get them all the way to Anchorage, plus look around for a parking space, nothing bad is going to happen, because, given his willingness to look at a map, they're never going to find their way out of Toledo anyway.

SEVENTEEN NAMES THAT MEAN EVERYTHING TO GIRLS

Ralph Lauren

Calvin Klein

Ortho-Gynol

Weight Watchers

Publishers Clearing House

Famous Amos

Tab

Tara

Hellmann's

Woolite

American Express

Mary Cunningham

Clinique

Arm & Hammer

Earl Grey

Jean Harris

Dr. Scholl

EIGHTEEN NAMES THAT MEAN SO MUCH TO GIRLS THAT THEY KNOW THEM JUST BY THEIR INITIALS

UPS

YSL

AAA

HBO

OB-GYN

M&M

E.T.

BLT

ASPCA

A&P

2BDR WBF

SWM

LAX

QE2

IRS

PMS

MBA

IBM

THE SPECIAL RELATIONSHIP BETWEEN GIRLS AND CATS

If girls chose their cats the way they choose their boyfriends and their stationery, they would always go with a Siamese, an Abyssinian, a white Persian, a blue Persian, or maybe a baby cheetah or an ocelot cub. Girls, however, do not choose their cats. They adopt them, they inherit them, they take them in, they allow cats to choose them. The girl model for the cat, in other words, is not the ideal mate but the self, and if girls see themselves as strays, or orphans, then they are likely to live with a scruffy street fighter that likes to nap on top of the row of books under the bedroom window. Unfortunately, the girl relationship with cats is not only deeply touching but immensely exploitable, and poor working girls who can barely afford the Kal Kan and their own cheese sandwiches and weak tea have now also been taught to require the latest Garfield, thereby no doubt underwriting some of the most stunning American revival architecture in the Hamptons, where publishing executives with Armani blazers and tennis elbow would just as soon have locusts as cats.

GIRLS AND DOGS

Boys harbor an ineradicable suspicion that cats are female and dogs are male, and if a girl has a dog, and particularly if she has a big dog such as a German shepherd or a St. Bernard or a Labrador retriever, then the dog is obviously a substitute for a boyfriend-lover and the girl is a closet lesbian. In fact, a girl might not be utterly unjustified in preferring a dog to a boyfriend-lover, because the average boyfriend-lover doesn't fetch or, for that matter, even show very much excitement when she walks through the door, let alone lap her face. For a girl, a small dog—a Pekinese or a Lhasa apso—is a cat that heels; a large dog is a burglar-alarm system that is actually enthusiastic about waking up out of a sound sleep and going for cigarettes no matter what the hour, with no grousing on the order of and-what-do-you-ever-do-for-me?

GIRLS AND ENDANGERED SPECIES

Girls may not lose an awful lot of sleep over the origin of species, but they do take an impassioned interest in the way species go out of business, and the fact that species can be endangered at all bears out everything that girls may ever have surmised about the bad faith of boys. Girls tend to think of nature as the place that Bambi and Dumbo and Elsa came out of the forest from; and they would gladly use their own bodies as shields to protect anything that is one-of-a-kind, or even merely approaching one-of-a-kind, particularly if it has just been hatched out of an egg and has to be fed with tweezers and an eyedropper. The fact that boys are attracted to one-of-a-kinds as a challenge to their marksmanship is probably responsible for the breakup of as many boy–girl relationships as the seashore–mountains dispute or Monday night football versus *I Love Lucy* reruns.

GIRLS AND COCKROACHES

In the girl imagination, cockroaches are the animate form of dirt, grease, and slime. Every splash of bacon grease not cleaned off of the wall, every crumb gone forever through the crevice between stove and counter top, every hair left in the bathtub drain —these, alive and nightstalking, are a cockroach infestation. Otherwise, a cockroach infestation is caused by a girl's having the unwisdom to move into an apartment next to a boy's apartment. Whatever the cause, cockroaches are a reflection of failure, the adult world's answer to a C− in home economics. The girl response to a cockroach infestation parallels exactly the pattern that psychologists have identified in the bereaved: shock, disbelief, denial, self-pity, acceptance, moving to a better building. Girls would react more aggressively to a cockroach attack, but they secretly believe that the average cockroach control product is itself a cockroach breeder.

GIRLS AND OTHER PEOPLE'S CHILDREN

Other people's children bring out some strange things in girls. A girl might, for example, go to the circus with her very best friend and the friend's five-year-old daughter, and when the mother goes to buy popcorn the girl will tell the child in a perfectly conversational way that the mother probably won't ever come back again. On another occasion, the same girl might tiptoe in on a baby while it's sleeping, sneak kisses on its fat baby legs, breathe in its sweet baby smell, then just sit around watching it as if it were some kind of miracle on the order of space travel or diet Coke.

GIRLS AND CHILDREN IN GENERAL

When a girl thinks about how she might one day have a child of her own, what intrigues her the most is the opportunity to reveal to the world the superiority of her taste by giving it the one perfect drop-dead name—Alexandra, Chloe, Clarissa, Tuck, or Ned, as the case may be. Girls often tell boys that they don't intend to have children, that as free spirits they'd much rather travel or devote themselves to aerospace engineering. In fact, girls figure they can have a child on the side, like Russian dressing, either before their career as a painter warms up or during a lull between appointments, on the nothing-human-is-alien-to-me principle. When a girl thinks about having a child in marriage, she of course expects that the child will stand by her through divorce proceedings and keep her company and giggle with her during the long winter nights while she's waiting for the date to turn up and the chocolate chip cookies to cool, because she's never really decided whether she wants to have a child or be a child herself.

WHY GIRLS HAVE TO HAVE *VOGUE* THE DAY IT COMES OUT

When a girl is under the spell of *Vogue,* her heart thrills at the certain knowledge that all the fabulous things in the world can be within her reach if she would only put more lipstick on, suck in her cheeks, and remember not to stand up too straight. A girl thinks: *I am a gorgeous thing with legs. Modern life requires ocelot skin. Italy is the birthplace of my soul.* When a girl is under the spell of *Vogue,* she believes herself to be the equal of endive, linen, Gore Vidal, Karl Lagerfeld, Hans Holbein, Virgil, and the right-nowness of yesterday and tomorrow and right now. The *Vogue* spell lasts for a couple of hours out of every month and wears off with no aftereffects other than the tossing of a scarf over one shoulder and a somewhat devil-may-care approach to mascara. The lifeless corpse of the magazine, however, lies around for several months until the night a girl uses it to bludgeon a cockroach, at which point she disposes of it immediately, at arm's length.

GIRLS AND *COSMO*

If *Vogue* addresses itself to the woman in a girl, *Cosmopolitan* addresses itself to the dental hygienist. What the dental hygienist wants to know is: Will he get the divorce? Will suicide make me any less desirable as a date? Can I wear black décolleté to the first night of my Stock Index Futures and Options course? Could I get the same answers by watching *Dallas?* As a girl gets older, she considers *Cosmo* farther and farther beneath her dignity, until she has a major boyfriend crisis, when every last cover line, not to mention the horoscope column and "Step Into My Parlor," seems to contain as much wisdom as the *I Ching*. Then she buys the magazine on the sly, sneaks it into her bedroom, remembers that the guy was always too short anyway and, finally, goes out and buys a copy of *Harper's Bazaar* to cleanse her palate.

MOTHERS AS GIRLS

Mothers are normally thought to be what girls turn into when they grow up and take on responsibility and offer themselves as candidates for elective office in Parents Against Sex and Violence on Television. In fact, though, mothers do not emerge out of girls in the same irreversible way that a butterfly emerges from a chrysalis. Mothers are girls stifled, girls under wraps, and the girl in them sometimes possesses the mother either by fits and seizures or by simple self-indulgence when nobody is looking. Mothers are girls when they sleep all night on the living room couch, when they sleep in their own bed but without taking all their clothes off, when they tell an untruth, when they ask to borrow ten dollars, when they go off by themselves in the afternoon to watch a John Travolta movie, when they have a second glass of wine, when they need to be brought around after a fit of petulance. When a mother gets caught being a girl, she has one intense, pleased, and embarrassed flare-up of girlishness and then she reverts to being even more of a mother, but only until the next time.

ON THE METTLE OF GIRLS

The principal resources that girls bring to an unaccommodating world are nerve, pluck, spunk, gameness, and bravura—as well as resourcefulness itself. The dilemma of girls is this: They want to live as richly as the Renaissance popes, they want to see the Tony Award-winning plays, they want to thrive rather than merely survive—yet it is at the level of mere survival that they are always being challenged. When a girl leaves her house in the morning, as dazzling a product of the human imagination as any canvas by Botticelli or Raphael, as outwardly carefree as the dance band aboard the *Titanic,* it never occurs to the people jostling her on the bus or vying with her for a taxi that she is full of desperate resolve: that the cat has just come down with polio, the rent is two weeks overdue, the boyfriend pawned her television set and left his farewell note in Magic Marker on her favorite silk dressing gown—indeed, the only thing standing between her and the bottom of the reservoir is the off-chance that she can talk the boss into reassigning her to a city where at least the *Mary Tyler Moore Show* reruns are on before two in the morning.

Living as they do without patronage or annuities, with only a thin line of moisturizer between themselves and the abyss, it is girls who embody the human spirit in our time. Given their hardiness, their adaptability, and their genius for constantly reinventing themselves, it is girls who are also likely to embody the human spirit when, several hundred years from now, the Peter Pan principle and the greenhouse effect are forgotten and the challenge is to find a decent rent-controlled apartment with a terrace overlooking the outer edges of space.